Metamorphosis

POLLY MORLAND spent fifteen years working as a documentary maker for the BBC, Channel 4 and the Discovery Channel. Her first book, *The Society of Timid Souls or, How to be Brave* won a Royal Society of Literature Jerwood Award and was longlisted for the Guardian First Book Award. Her second, *Risk Wise: Nine Everyday Adventures* was written in conjunction with The School of Life, where Polly is a faculty member. She lives in the Wye Valley with her husband and three sons.

www.pollymorland.com

Metamorphosis

How and Why We Change

POLLY MORLAND

P

PROFILE BOOKS

This paperback edition published in 2017

First published in Great Britain in 2016 by
PROFILE BOOKS LTD
3 Holford Yard
Bevin Way
London WC1X 9HD
www.profilebooks.com

1 3 5 7 9 10 8 6 4 2

Typeset in Garamond by MacGuru Ltd
Printed and bound in Great Britain by
CPI Group (UK) Ltd, Croydon CR0 4YY

A CIP catalogue record for this book is available from the British Library.

ISBN 978 1 78125 413 4
eISBN 978 1 78283 137 2

For H,
who changed everything

CONTENTS

Omnia mutantur, nihil interit
Everything changes, but nothing is lost.

Ovid, *Metamorphoses* XV

A NOTE ON SOURCES

In the interests of readability, ellipses have not been used within quotations from the interviews that appear throughout this book, but great care has been taken throughout to remain true to the speaker's meaning. A few names have been changed to protect privacy. Each contributor's testimony has been reported in good faith and while facts have been checked wherever possible, the text relies chiefly upon their accounts of dates, times and events.

PREFACE

Yesterday afternoon, as winter twilight descended, I sat with my children at the darkening kitchen table watching on a laptop as Donald Trump was sworn in as 45th President of the United States of America. It is not often that you get to watch change happen, consciously and in real-time, its screen-glow on your face. The spectacle was compelling. For a full hour, not one of us said a word.

The political paroxysms of 2016, preceding that Washington ceremony, came hard on the heels of my work on this book. Three years in the making, *Metamorphosis* was conceived and written with little idea of the political tectonics that lay ahead. First published just a fortnight after Trump became the presumptive Republican nominee and a month before the Brexit vote here in the UK, the book was my response to a sense that desire for change was in the air, simultaneously urgent and amorphous. It was not that I foresaw the coming political storm, much less the tide of ugliness and uncertainty it would bring with it, but that everywhere I looked there seemed to be a thirst for personal transformation. Even when there was not much in the way of clarity about which aspect of their lives people wished to change – and this was a key feature of the phenomenon – there persisted a feeling within many of us that our very identity was at stake. It was contagious, this sense that we had a right, even a duty, to realise the person we wished to be, the life we deserved to lead.

The point is that it was tempting, back then, to regard this yearning for change as personal, not political. Except that it *was* political. It was personal *and* political. These things, the individual and the society in which he or she lives, the private and the public, are of course connected. Indeed the political turmoil of these last weeks and months, the clamour of division and dissent, arguably sprang from this legion of desires for individual change.

Which is no reason to stop believing in change itself – quite the reverse. It is the very reason we must work harder than ever at honing our understanding of change, at learning to be not reactive but imaginative about the kind of future we want and why we want it. Indeed the extent of our self-determination, both personally and politically, meets its testing point when we try to change either ourselves or our societies. That to me is as good a reason as any to show, as I have tried to do in this book, that yes, we can change, we do change, but heaven knows, we need to think about the what and the how.

We do not know where we will go from here or what on earth will come next. What we do know is this: that directing our hunger for change wisely is more important today than perhaps at any other time in the last half century. I am not merely saying be careful what you wish for, nor arguing that stasis is desirable or even possible. What I am saying is that it is not enough simply to want change either for yourself or your society. Indeed we have a burning responsibility as individuals, as citizens and as a society, to think long and think hard about *why* we want to change, *what* we want to change and *how* it might be done. Everyone in the following pages did that – and even in days as strange and turbulent as these, their stories give me hope.

Polly Morland
21 January 2017

INTRODUCTION

This book is an experiment in a way. And you, the reader, are invited to join in. No lab coat will be required or protective goggles. There will be no need for Bunsen burners or test-tubes, no computer programs capable of crunching large bodies of data, no microscopes, telescopes or horoscopes – although the future will be very much on our minds. Instead, this will be an intimate, personal affair, and all you need bring along by way of equipment is your imagination. So please, turn it loose from beneath the bell jar of your mind, let it flutter about the room and we can begin.

The experiment, in the loosest sense of the word, is about change: why we want it, whether it is possible, how we achieve it and what follows afterwards. To that extent, it is about the central story of our lives and how our imagination shapes what we hope for, what we fear. For which of us would not change something about our lives if we could? We labour daily under an astonishing range of cravings for transformations large and small. We yearn to go from fat to thin or sad to happy, bored to fulfilled, angry to peaceful, lonely to loved, steering our days from confusion to clarity, disillusionment to new meaning, fear to safety or failure to success.

Our culture is one in which, more than ever before, we feel entitled to change our experiences and ourselves to fit with our dreams and aspirations. That option to change, to be the author of one's own life, matters. It defines the extent of our freedom, entwining our most cherished ideas about equality, democracy, autonomy. Yet all too often we are flummoxed as to how to go about it – so much so that we become sitting ducks for a volley of quick-fix change solutions, from self-help books to diet plans, tranquil retreats to motivational mobile apps.

But this book is not about the quick fix. It is not about step plans or silver bullets or proscriptive methodologies. There is no desire here to add to that heap. Instead, we shall ask four central questions about change and answer them through real people who have changed and are changing. The experiment is about the power of their stories to open our minds, to show us new ways of thinking about change for ourselves.

Of course, the flip side of our frequent bewilderment about how to change is that everything – and everyone – changes all the time. Our spinning world is never still. Our rivers, as the ancient Greek philosopher Heraclitus observed more than two and a half millennia ago, they flow. We grow up. We grow old. We learn. We evolve, devolve, revolve. We get new jobs. We move house. We fall in love. And out of love. We make decisions. We change our minds. We become parents. People dear to us die. We are sad and then we are happy again. Old friends depart or fall from favour. New friends appear and make us smile. The sun sets. The sun rises. And tomorrow is a new day, every day, for everyone.

Heraclitus' famous point about the river was made obliquely in a fragment of manuscript that is frequently misinterpreted. It was not, as is often quoted, that because the waters change, you can never step into the same river twice.

Rather, it was that some things are what they are *because* they change. It is only a river *because* it flows. We are only human beings, not in spite of change, but *because* we change.

The truth is that we are better at this than we think. Indeed, we are masters of the change that drives life. We are endlessly adaptive and inventive, far less tractable than we assume or often feel. This is the *sine qua non* built into our life cycle and our very biology. The lingering childhood that is exclusive to the human animal is inextricably linked to the unique capacity of our brains for learning and for imaginative flight. This is what powers our ability to change, both individually and collectively, while remaining at some fundamental level the same thing, the same river, the same person. Change – as an unfolding process rather than a sovereign remedy – is *who we are*.

That is why the metamorphosis in this book is not that of the Roman poet Ovid's dreamscape, where people are turned (involuntarily) into animals, trees, birds, flowers, whirlpools in the ocean, constellations of stars in the sky. Indeed, you need a strong stomach for Ovid's classical catalogue of rape, suicide, incest, cannibalism and mutilation, in which sundry unrequited or unwholesome desires are met with violent punishment and fantastical transformation. Nor is the metamorphosis in this book that of Kafka's alienated salesman Gregor Samsa, as he scrabbles about as a beetle, or some say a cockroach, in his family's apartment. No, instead, one could do worse than turn to Eric Carle's *The Very Hungry Caterpillar*. Because the world that concerns us here is the one in which myriad small miracles of change and continuity take place every day. This is the world where caterpillars become beautiful butterflies and where people can and do change in extraordinary ways.

For metamorphosis is all around us, although within human beings it often takes longer than a few days. In

3

exploring why we *want* to change, we will see how the natural forces of external flux meet the spark of human agency in the desire to be master of our own lives. In examining the extent to which we *can* change in body and mind, we will discover the importance of choosing which changes to make, which doors to open. In unfolding *how* we change, we will find that we can make it happen not by scuttling the mystery of the process but by harnessing that mystery with pragmatism. And in asking what it is to *be changed*, what follows and sustains transformation, we will learn how resilient and yet how flexible our identity is, even to the most profound metamorphosis.

Most important of all, we shall meet a handful of remarkable people, whose stories contain some powerful change medicine. And this is the crux. There are countless blueprints for change out there: some of them daft, some of them the fruit of many years of sober empirical research. Yet not one of the people in the pages that follow – and this was not the objective but the key surprise of the research process – *not one of them* pursued change or found it through a single paradigm, a particular self-help book or step plan or therapeutic intervention. Yes, they read, they took advice, they explored established wisdoms and talking cures, but, above all, each was inspired in one way or another and each built their own change process. It came from within and *they did it*, no one else. Sometimes they struggled. Often they made mistakes. Frequently they avoided change, doubted it was even possible, but in the end, one day, one week, one year, they proved themselves wrong. They did it. It was about agency powered by imagination, by tenacity and often by courage.

So if you are in search of a handy manual on how to Change Your Life in Seven Days, you had better look elsewhere. But if you would like to understand what change is, how and why it really happens – if you would care to experiment with whether these stories can move you to think afresh about metamorphosis in your own life – then please read on. And by all means, start building, start imagining. Yes, even start changing, like the nineteen fluttering butterflies that follow here.

PART I

WHY DO WE WANT
TO CHANGE?

1

ON GROWING UP

Overlooking a quiet street of suburban houses, with neat front lawns and heathery hillside beyond, Police Sergeant Coxon sits in a tidy, plain living-room. He is not in uniform today, but his bearing is straight and a little formal, almost as though he were. On the floor there are two large baskets overflowing with soft toys, plastic trucks and those fabric picture books designed to withstand chewing by their readership. Over the hours that follow, these baskets periodically emit an incongruous coda of melody, a bleat or a moo, a tinny siren.

Sergeant Coxon has just come off night shift and his baby son is teething. He apologises for being 'a bit exhausted' and smiles, making a little circle on the closed lids of both eyes with surprisingly delicate, tapering fingertips.

Recently promoted to sergeant after a decade as a front-line constable, Coxon's beat is the southern hub of the Edinburgh urban area. There he and another sergeant run one of five emergency response teams, serving 120,000 people, from both affluent and deprived communities. His conversation is punctuated with glimpses of what he calls the 'gritty' side of his work. Suicides, murder, sweeping brain matter off the tarmac after car crashes, the knock on an unsuspecting door with terrible news.

'Appalling things happen to people on a daily basis,' he says, the decorous precision of his Edinburgh accent taming the chaos for a moment, 'but you learn to deal with it and it's made me a better person, being a police officer. My mind has been broadened immeasurably, my insight into what really goes on out in the world.' He glances to the street outside, where a man is whistling as he washes his car. 'It's actually given me great faith in human nature and it's essential work.'

Everyone is changed in some way, small or large, by the job they do, the particular window on the world it affords, but that is only in part what Edmund Coxon's story is about. For insofar as any of us is *meant* to be one thing or the other, Ed, as people call him, was not *meant* to be a police officer. Indeed, the journey that brought him here to his black uniform and highly polished shoes is an immaculate example of why so many of us want to change: that confluence of organic, natural change process – call it growing up, if you will – with the sharp kick of individual agency that underpins all deliberate acts of transformation. It is a tale of how the reasons why we want to change, myriad as they are, all stem from a desire to be the author of our own lives and of how that can sometimes lead us to take on the most unexpected new forms.

On the subject of growing up, biologists have long argued that what happens to us during the transition from juvenility into adulthood is a change of body and mind more profound than any other we experience. A few have even maintained that the hormonally controlled differentiation that takes the human animal through adolescence could reasonably be considered a variation of the biological 'miracle' of metamorphosis. It is a hypothesis that strikes an intuitive chord: we all know that the process of growing up, even well beyond our teens, changes who we are at some level. Indeed achieving our adult selves, learning to take control of our lives, often entails something akin to a metamorphosis, a profound transformation of our mode of being in the world.

The only visible trace today of Ed's big change, his metamorphosis, is propped up in a far corner of his dining-room – the cocoon of a black violin case. The instrument inside, as Ed mentions with pride, once belonged to the legendary violinist and conductor Sir Neville Marriner, founder of the Academy of St Martin in the Fields. For, strange to tell, before Ed Coxon became a police constable, he was a classical violinist with a career that saw him play in some of the finest orchestras in the world. Moreover, it was a life carved out for him and by him from his earliest childhood. A violinist was what Ed Coxon was always meant to be.

The son of a university classics professor and a singing teacher, Ed grew up in a house where music dominated. His little bedroom was next door to the room where his mother taught, with its grand piano, shelves of scores and gramophone records of operas, symphonies, quartets.

'I was just enveloped in music', he says. 'It was' – he thinks for a moment – 'a pre-existing condition. It never occurred to me I would do anything other than be a musician.'

A chorister from the age of six in a specialist music school, Ed took up the violin at nine and had an immediate, dazzling aptitude for it. 'Even when I didn't have the instrument in my hands, I would play tunes on my fingers. I just had music going on in my head all the time.'

He describes with almost religious reverence going to a concert a few years later by the Chamber Orchestra of Europe in the vast domed bulk of the Usher Hall, just below Edinburgh Castle. Looking down from his seat high above, Ed had thought, he now recollects with teenage intensity, 'God, I want to do that. I've got to play in that orchestra. *That is all I want to do.*'

The ease with which the police sergeant switches from talking about murder and car smashes to re-inhabiting the musical passions of his youthful self seems to show how unconditional that love once was. Yet it would be the tough realities of the real, grown-up world, both in and outside the music profession, which would begin to erode the young violinist's idealism and his vocation.

At just seventeen Ed went to music college in London and sure enough, by the age of twenty he was playing with the Chamber Orchestra of Europe, whom he had heard in Edinburgh that decisive day. A promising career now unfolded. He toured the concert halls of the world, played for legendary conductors. Ed names them still with hushed reverence – Abbado, Bernstein, Doráti – like so many holy men. Meanwhile, he was growing up in other ways too. He offers a photograph of himself from the late 1980s, a moodily handsome young man dressed in concert black, his violin propped on one wrist, the very image of talent and confidence. 'The only crises I suffered in those days were with girls' and Ed laughs a little mirthlessly. Without offering much more in the way of detail – his wife is in the room next door – he mentions that at twenty-two his girlfriend at the time fell pregnant. The couple hastily married and the baby was born.

'I was too young, really', he says with a barely perceptible shake of his head. 'And this was the point at which I realised life wasn't quite so rosy, because I now was going to have

to do things for other people' – he taps his knee with a fingertip as though bringing himself to account – 'a child, a
wife, bills, taxation. I've got to get through these auditions,
because I'm responsible for this. I've got bills to pay.'

On cue, a toy buried in one of the baskets pipes up with
a few bars of *Pop Goes the Weasel* and, giving it a little kick,
Ed explains that this is when the doubt began. 'Well, maybe
it wasn't a doubt so much as a desire', he says. 'I didn't doubt
that I wanted to continue in music, but I had the first seeds
of desire to learn other things in life and that these were
things that I possibly had a duty to understand.'

The marriage lasted just eighteen months, but the subtle
shift of outlook that had accompanied Ed's transition to
fatherhood refused to go away. Instead, the questioning
spiralled.

'I felt like there was this disconnect between me and the
outside world,' he says, ' inhabiting, as I had for many years,
this wonderful parallel universe of music and now I wanted
rid of that insularity and to actually have a look, see what's
going on out in the real world. Because how connected to
the real world is all this?' Ed holds an imaginary violin in the
air for a moment, which then evaporates in his hands as he
shrugs and says, 'I began to feel that it's not.'

So one day, unbeknownst to his colleagues in the orchestra, Ed sat down in his Brixton lodgings and wrote the
opening words of a new story for himself. Inked into blank
boxes, the words filled an application form to become a
Special Constable with the Metropolitan Police, the Con-
stabulary's part-time, unpaid volunteer force. And here
came Revelation Number One: a reply came by return,
inviting Ed for an interview.

'It'd just been a kind of experiment, like dipping my
elbow into the bathwater, you know? But now I thought,
Oh my God.' Ed beams for the first time all morning.

'Somebody has an interest in what I can offer. And that was the first chink of light where I thought I can be something other than a musician.'

All the same, Ed declined.

He smiles, holding aloft two pale hands. 'I thought, *No, I can't. It's too dangerous. What if I hurt my fingers?*' And off he went to rehearsal.

Anyone vexed by questions of why we want to change – what is reason enough? – and how on earth to begin, would do well to picture Edmund Coxon walking through the drizzle on the Brixton Road that day, violin in hand. On paper, nothing was any different. Yet the chorus of desires within him, all its complex internal counterpoint – that 'why' of change – is where transformation itself quietly stirs into life.

An eminent mid-century psychiatrist, Alfred Benjamin, makes the point with an anecdote from his own life. Walking home from his Boston consulting rooms one evening, Dr Benjamin was approached by a stranger who asked him directions to a particular street. Benjamin cordially obliged, with a series of detailed lefts and rights that would lead the stranger, without delay, to where he wanted to go. The man paid close attention, nodding and confirming the specifics – 'Left, you say? And then right?' – before thanking the kind doctor and bidding him good night. Walking away with a new purpose in his step, he set off *up* the street instead of, as Benjamin had carefully outlined, *down* it.

'You're heading in the wrong direction', the doctor called out.

'Yes, I know,' replied the man over his shoulder, 'but I'm not quite ready yet.' And back he went the way he had come.

There is little academic consensus on a grand narrative of why we change or how, but on one thing all psychologists and philosophers seem to agree: that inner change does not begin in an orderly fashion at an appointed hour and with rational, coherent, decisive action. It does not leave a platform like a train. Instead, like the stranger in Alfred Benjamin's neighbourhood, even if you have worked out that there is a journey to be made, even if you have an idea of where it is you wish to go, you may not yet be quite ready to set off. But you have – and this is important – commenced the journey. Amid the countless reasons out there in the world for wanting to change, you have identified the universal departure point: autonomy. And in the process, you have begun to change.

Suffice to say, Ed Coxon did not become a Special Constable and seven or eight more years of fine music-making ensued. In the early 1990s and now in his late twenties, Ed joined an eminent string ensemble, but soon found himself embroiled in an ill-advised love affair with the artistic director. 'Business and pleasure,' he says, looking at his feet, 'a very dangerous mix.' When the liaison turned sour, Ed was, in his words, 'unceremoniously dumped' from both relationship and job. 'It was the first time I'd experienced negative politics in music and I was very offended, very upset. And that was very much a turning-point.'

Ed moved into session music and his disillusionment snowballed. There were high points – recording with Pink Floyd, two James Bond soundtracks, a private concert with Paul McCartney – but something had broken. He felt worn out and jaded. The focus and drive of his youth now dwindled to a bitterness that jarred with the yearning that had grown within him to lead a more authentic life, to do something 'real'.

'This is the point at which I started to think much more seriously, *Well, what else is there?*' Ed says it again, slicing the air on each word. 'Because I just didn't want to become that embittered person and there was every chance I might.'

Here then was Revelation Number Two: that if you are not careful, you may turn into somebody you do not wish to be. Within that realisation the seeds of taking control, of active change, were sown. Because, of course, the maelstrom of growing up, long beyond adolescence, does not just bring disillusionment. It also brings independence; it brings choice and the possibility of acting on that choice.

'The mind', the philosopher and father of modern psychology, William James, wrote in 1890, 'is at every stage a theatre of simultaneous possibilities.' You choose, according to James, by comparing, selecting or suppressing them with the laser beam of your attention. Perturbed by what remaining a professional musician might do to him as a person, Ed now returned his attention to the possibility of police work. A full decade on from the first twinge of desire to look beyond the music of his childhood, he began in earnest to picture an entirely different life. Law enforcement seemed more than ever to offer him something he was missing: a way to 'distinguish between right and wrong and good and evil and black and white and up and down and left and right'. He laughs as he says this, but he clearly still believes it.

All the reasons to change, all those simultaneous possibilities, were now there for the choosing. The final impetus to action itself would boil over from a more universal milestone in the maturing process – the death of his father in 2001, when Ed was thirty-five.

'Realising I could never get my dad back', he says, 'was the point at which I thought, *Well, now I'm the only one who's responsible for what happens in my life*. I saw that change was inevitable and imperative for me, because' – he searches for the words – 'well, life is in session. This isn't a rehearsal.'

Without delay Ed prepared what he calls, with a grin, 'my renaissance'. Within months of his father's death, he had applied to join the Lothian and Borders Police, back in his home city of Edinburgh.

'I remember going over the application meticulously', says Ed, smiling broadly, 'and thinking that I had to keep this a secret, because I would be derided by most of my colleagues and I might start to question myself. And I didn't want to question myself. So I told nobody. Not even my mother.'

Ed travelled 'totally incognito' to Scotland for the first interview. On getting through, he told only his mother and within days his London house was on the market. Finally, in the spring of 2003 and to howls of 'You're crazy! You're mad!' from colleagues and friends, Edmund Coxon ceased to be a professional musician and from that day on he was a police officer.

'I don't recall that I got any positive response from anybody', he says. 'It was just incredulity. Because the classical music world, it's inhabited by the privileged and the few, so why would you disembark from that to something that's not nearly so cosy and well paid? Well, I'll tell you: just for honesty's sake. Just because it's real.'

Now, as if he has said everything he needed to say, Ed moves to get up, pausing only to add, 'Once I was in the job, I knew I'd done the right thing. I felt totally rejuvenated. It really was a renaissance, a rebirth and I was in control of it.' He nods toward the instrument in the dining-room. 'I do occasionally miss playing the violin, but not very often, and yes, before you ask, I do love the police as much as I love music. I think I'm still a musician. I still play tunes on my fingers, but I'm also a police officer.' And he smiles and puts on his coat.

Driving to collect Ed's two-year-old from nursery through Edinburgh's steep, rain-streaked thoroughfares, you pass suburban bungalows, council estates, elegant Georgian town houses. There are shoppers with their hoods up, the homeless propped in doorways, suited office workers hailing cabs, schoolboys smoking at a bus stop. An old lady peers out from behind a net curtain, a mother tugs down the rain shield on her child's pushchair, all of them part of the community served by Ed and the officers of the Edinburgh South hub. This, you realise, is what he meant by real life. It makes sense, somehow, of why Ed changed.

Meanwhile, he is talking about the pieces of music that marked particular milestones when he was growing up. There are a few, but he offers one in particular that will, he says, 'remain with me for the rest of my days'. It is by Richard Strauss and is scored for twenty-three solo strings. Ed first played it here in Edinburgh as a teenager.

Its name? *Metamorphosen*.

2

ON REDEMPTION

Edmund Coxon, so he said that day, was only ever once truly frightened during his police work. Questioning a suspect already in custody for a number of brutally violent offences, Ed recalled how knowing the awful things this man had done conspired with his tough-guy demeanour in the interview room to terrifying effect.

'But I know that this man wasn't always a bad man,' Ed said, 'and that when he started out he was as good and as pure as I was the day I was born. Something had happened to him to make him so accustomed to doing bad things, to make that the arena in which he felt most comfortable.' And Ed visibly shuddered.

Every one of us, of course, begins life with a blank page, but once we get under way, accountability for our actions is fundamental to our very identity. Even the metamorphosed butterfly is the same single individual as the caterpillar. And this is of material importance to our experience of change.

It is a point made somewhat eccentrically by the ancient Greek wag Epicharmus Comicus of Syracuse, in a fragment of a not entirely side-splitting joke from the fifth century BC. It goes (something) like this:

Alpha has lent Beta ten silver drachma, which Beta has failed to repay. Alpha collars Beta one day and asks for his money back. But instead of giving Alpha either the money or a straight answer, Beta draws a handful of pebbles from his pocket.

'See these pebbles?' asks Beta.

Alpha nods.

'If I add one more' – and Beta does – 'is it the same pile?'

'Of course not,' says Alpha.

'And if I take a pebble away' – which Beta does, with a flourish – 'is it the same pile? Or different?'

'Different,' says Alpha. 'What's your point?'

'Ah,' says Beta, sagely, 'now consider men in this way too. Do we not grow and also decline?'

Alpha nods again testily.

'You see!' says Beta. 'We are all changing all the time and that which has changed must be different. So we are neither of us the men we were when you lent me that ten drachma –' and there the crumbled edge of the papyrus spirited Alpha's punchline away into oblivion.

The point of the joke, of course, is that Beta's specious argument leads to naught but unpaid debts and quite possibly broken noses. Indeed, however we may want to change, however we may succeed in doing so, we can never quite untether ourselves from the things we have done, the tenners we have borrowed in the past. You cannot simply declare yourself a new entity. And yet that in many ways unreasonable desire to do so – to wipe the slate clean and begin again – can nevertheless sometimes prove a powerful catalyst for change.

Freedom. Ray Bishop has the word tattooed in an ornate Baroque script up the inside of his forearm, little curlicues of ornamentation splicing the blue tracks of his veins. Freedom is why Ray Bishop wanted to change.

'Because that's what I craved so much', he says, with one arm out of his black parka, his sleeve pushed up and fist outstretched on the table, alongside a soapy-looking cappuccino going cold in its cup.

'And when I say that, it's not the freedom from the film – what is it – the one with Mel Gibson as William Wallace?'

'*Braveheart.*'

'Yeah, where he cries out "Freedom!" But no, to me freedom became very important because I was so institutionalised; if I wasn't in prison, I was in rehab. I couldn't function in society. So really the freedom I was always looking for was freedom from myself. I felt like I was a person I didn't want to be. I never wanted to be me. Even as a kid, I wanted to be *you*. I never wanted what I had, I wanted what *you* had. I never had much of a family. I wanted *your* family' – there is an uncomfortably personal pause – 'I wanted freedom from the parts of myself that I found most objectionable, the parts I tried to snuff out with drug use, the anger, the hate, the bitterness, the part of me that felt unworthy, unlovable; because that was how I felt at my core. When you peeled the lousy onion, that was Ray at the core.'

The source of this powerful reason to change, Raymond Bishop, is a wiry, edgy man with the flattened features of a fighter. Sitting here mid-morning in a dingy pub in a provincial town centre, he looks older than his forty years. Once described by another south London face as being 'as game as a bag of rabid pit bulls', Ray has spent more than half of his life in and out of prison – 'I couldn't stay out for more than two or three months', he says. A career criminal with a long history of violence and addiction, his last prison sentence, ten years for people-smuggling, was compounded by a violent escape from the courtroom during his trial. Thereafter classed as a Category A prisoner, he was incarcerated in a succession of maximum-security jails.

'I've lived a very violent life,' he says, softly, 'and I've been a very dangerous man. Most of it I regret. I progressed to –' he picks up the coffee cup and puts it down again – 'a moral waste ground where there's probably not much I wouldn't have done and by the very end of my drug-using and my criminality, I was quite capable of murder. I can't remember half the people I've harmed' and he glances out of the window at the shoppers walking past.

Recalling Ed Coxon's point that no individual is born bad, this terrible life that Ray has lived is one that seems to exemplify two distinct and dramatic forms of change: one the spiralling corruption of his character, the other an arduous voyage of redemption back from the shores of Hell. It is this arc of story that Ray has come here to narrate; his much-vaunted freedom seems to depend on it.

And you can understand why. This kind of transformation is one that society habitually regards with scepticism, which often only perpetuates the cycle. This, perhaps, is why Ray is happy to talk with such bruising candour to a total stranger with a voice recorder and a notebook. Telling the story, as for others we shall meet anon, is part of the redemption; it drowns out the background noise of incredulity.

The study of criminal desistence, of why and how some people break patterns of recidivism, is an academic field in its own right. Yet at its heart sits something of a problem. Measuring, or indeed pursuing, a change that is characterised chiefly by an absence – less offending, less harm, less risk – is a slippery task indeed, offering little idea of what the desired end-state should look like. Yet aspiration and hope have been proven to be of material importance in offender rehabilitation. That is why a number of influential psychologists and sociologists in the field have worked to identify and formalise the established conventions of so-called 'redemption narratives' such as Ray's. A valuable paradigm for change encompassing both behaviour and identity, these narratives plot a well-worn course. The blame is placed on dysfunctional childhoods for the degeneration of behaviour that follows; this is the organic change. Then comes the external trigger for remorse, the turning-point revelation that sparks a new sense of purpose, prompting the long, meandering journey home. The happy ending comes with the final arrival at the new, better self, now capable of taking responsibility for its actions, the whole yarn a kind of gritty modern-world *Odyssey* with the rehabilitated criminal as Homeric hero. Even when the truth is somewhat messier than that, these stories, so experts on desistence argue, serve an important practical purpose. They are useful fictions, if you will, that help people to seek better lives.

And Ray Bishop's is a classic of the genre – not that he would see it as a fiction in any way. He has taken authorship of every word and passionately so. He laughs, he weeps, he pounds the table to make his point. Whatever things Ray has done in the past, whatever lies he has told, his story comes across powerfully as one now told in good faith.

So sure enough, the spiral downwards, according to Ray, started young. 'I do believe,' he says, 'we are all products of our environment. Any psychologist, should I go out and commit murder tomorrow, they'd blame my childhood.' He is glaring at a man who has selected from the empty pub the next immediate table at which to strike up a loud, animated conversation on his mobile phone. Ray narrows his eyes at him and continues with an account of a miserable, deprived upbringing: the violent, alcoholic father who abandoned them, the 'cruel' stepfather who met any vulnerability with a cuff around the head, the mother who 'didn't do feelings', the hunger, the truancy, the rising sense of inferiority, alienation and sometimes outright panic that Ray masked first by making common cause with the troublemakers on his housing estate and before long by getting out of his head, 'literally', he says, on drugs. While the man at the next table guffaws and bellows, oblivious to Ray's scowls, he adds, 'So I've got no memories that I would call a happy childhood, not one, but I've got plenty of being told I'm bad, I'm just like my father, I've got "Bishop blood". And, well, water finds its own level, doesn't it?' With a jerk of his head toward the man on the phone, he adds, 'Come on, he's fucking giving me the hump' – and then softly – 'and I want to have a fag. Is that alright?'

Outside in the frost-nipped concrete of the pub garden, Ray describes how the lawlessness escalated, how self-perpetuating that gang culture can be, how it resets the moral norms.

'I'm not going to deny that I did get a buzz off certain aspects of it, the financial reward, the adrenaline', he says, sprinkling tobacco into a black liquorice paper, 'but the crimes did get worse and there was a lot of violence involved. I'm ashamed to admit I have blood on my hands and that's where the real conscience started to creep in' – Ray strikes a match – 'at night-time' – and he takes a long pull on his cigarette. 'I started to have nightmares and I think the fact that I started using the kinds of drugs I did, heroin and stuff, was a way of trying to snuff out that guilt.'

Ray devotes long portions of the testimony that follows to what he calls his 'internal conflict': the 'soft, loving child' and the 'monster' nevertheless 'plagued' by a conscience that 'ate away at me in bite-size pieces until I had no self worth left'. Ray spits these last few words out as though he cannot stand the taste of them in his mouth. The fact that what he calls 'the bad side' so often won, Ray attributes to his drug addiction. 'It turns you into something that you don't want to be', he says, eyes wide, and for a moment you catch a glimpse of a nightmarish inner world.

Yet for Ray Bishop it was out of this struggle and the remorse it fostered that the very beginnings of his desire to change were kindled. By his mid-twenties, when he had already been in and out of prison a number of times, a handful of Ray's friends had died, in quick succession, of heroin overdoses. Ray 'finally started to admit to myself how unhappy I was'. He applied through the probation service and got a place at a drug rehab centre. 'But it was unsuccessful', he says, the butt of the cigarette now flapping from his lower lip. 'I honestly believed that I would just wake up one morning and I'd be a different person'. He detaches the butt and flicks it away. 'At times I felt like there was this light on the horizon like something good was going to happen, but it never did.'

But change of this sort does not happen *to* you; it is something you *do*. So the cycle of violence and crime and prison and drugs continued. Round and round. Round and round. When on trial in 2000 for involvement in a people-smuggling ring, Ray attacked his guard in the secure dock of Maidstone Crown Court. His weapon? The casing of a Bic pen which he had chewed in half, filled with blackcurrant jam from a prison sandwich and finished with the point of a paper-clip from his court file to simulate a blood-filled syringe. He threatened to stick it in the guard's throat. A minute later he walked out of the courtroom, locking them in behind him, judge and all, and spent several days on the run before being recaptured.

Ray says that glimpsing the news report on the TV about his escape, with his police mug shot and a warning not to approach this dangerous man, was one key moment of realising 'the demon I'd become'. Another came when, now reclassified as a Category A prisoner, Ray found himself at HMP Long Lartin, one of five maximum-security prisons in the UK. Ray was to be held on the secure wing, along with thirty other men, 'most of them murderers,' says Ray with clear distaste, 'some of them serial killers, psychopaths, the people you read about in newspapers. And that was a stark realisation' – he rolls another cigarette – 'you know, looking around thinking, *I don't belong here. I shouldn't be here. What the fuck am I doing here?*' This last question is quite loud and the barman who is clearing a nearby table hurries inside, glancing back as he goes through the patterned glass of the door. 'It was at that moment,' Ray goes on, 'I told myself I've got to change.' He says it again. 'I've got to change. I'm not geared up for this life. I won't survive this life. I don't want to be here for the rest of my life. I've got to be worth more.'

This revelation seems to have reignited Ray's sense of agency. And it served as a fulcrum for the change process that then took him through the rest of his lengthy sentence. Changing with a capital 'C' was how he spent his time behind bars. Task number one? To get clean of drugs. That he accomplished within the first few months. Task number two? Education.

Ray had been psychometrically tested as part of his Category A status and it turned out that he has a high IQ. This is a fact of which he clearly remains proud. He mentions it over and over again. Over the years of incarceration, he got a first-class Open University degree and a Masters in psychology. Getting high marks in university essays became, he says, 'my new buzz, my new addiction. I discovered' – he grins – 'that I am a very intelligent man.' Ray's repetition of this is more than idle boasting; of all things, here is a part of the new story clearly worth reinforcing, a key element of the man Ray wanted to become.

'What I wanted to change most was my attitude towards the world. I wanted to be happy and be able to face the world drug-free, look it in the eye and say, "You know what? I'm doing the best I can."' Some of Ray's criminal friends from his early life had managed to move away from crime, so as Ray says, 'I knew change was possible, but I had to admit that I couldn't do it all by myself and that I needed help.'

Ray applied and, after rigorous assessment, was accepted for admission to HMP Grendon in Buckinghamshire, the only prison in the UK with a therapeutic regime and an explicit change agenda. It is no coincidence that, as he waited for transfer to Grendon, Ray chose to have 'Freedom' tattooed on his arm.

So unfolded three years of intense group therapy alongside some of the most feared characters within the British penal system, all of them, says Ray, 'desperately seeking change'. There was zero tolerance from the inmates of drugs: one strike and you were out. Zero tolerance of so-called 'ticket workers' too – lifers who saw Grendon as an opportunity to increase their chances of parole but had little interest in change. 'Because one bad apple in a fruit bowl', says Ray, 'tends to turn the rest.'

While the psychologists chipped away at correcting cognitive deficits, the faulty thinking that leads to and perpetuates persistent offending, for Ray it was the kindness of one particular prison officer called Paul Johnson that proved more transformative than anything else.

'Johnson was a father figure to me for the three years I was there. He'd come and sit beside me in my cell, put his arm round me and say, "Listen, it's going to be alright, you know. It's going to be alright." And I never had –' Ray's voice begins to wobble and he scrabbles in his pocket for the tobacco, whispering – 'I've never had that. I think throughout my entire childhood I think that's all I ever wanted, you know?' He swipes at a tear in the corner of one eye with a stubby thumb. 'I think if I'd have had that, I don't think I would have turned into the person that I did. That man has done more to stop people like me coming out of prison and committing murder than any man alive, if you ask me. You keep me in the company of people like that and the real Ray shines through.' And he rolls the cigarette in silence.

Raymond Bishop came out of prison in 2006; he got a job, won a boxing title, met a girl and, eight law-abiding years later, sitting here in the pub, he declares himself a changed man.

'I like the man I am today,' he says, 'and I do very much consider myself the leopard that changed his spots. I'm a living example of that and I will fiercely guard it, but I won't take it for granted because the journey's been very, very long and it's going to be never ending I know, so I take each day as it comes and each day the important thing for me is that I don't harm society. I try to contribute to life and I just don't feel the urge to be violent any more. It's gone.'

'Does that feel like the freedom you have written down your arm?'

'Very much so,' says Ray, 'very much so. That hunger for change fed me to change. And every day I tell myself I'm a good person, I'm a good person. It's self-fulfilling.'

'Time', mused Blaise Pascal, in Thought No. 122 of his celebrated *Pensées*, 'heals pain and quarrels because we change. We are no longer the same persons; neither the offender nor the offended are themselves any more.' The seventeenth-century theologian's words, although he was not contemplating prison time of course, seem to reprise the spurious argument in that ancient rib-tickler of Epicharmus. Yet, in the real world of criminal justice, responsibility for past actions rolls on.

In 2014, some months after that meeting in the pub, Ray Bishop wrote his story down for real, publishing a memoir of what he called 'my fight for redemption'. It seems that the book jogged a few unwelcome memories. Ray was arrested soon after, having been recognised by witnesses to two armed robberies committed more than twenty years earlier and a decade prior to his years of transformation. He pleaded guilty and began another five-year prison sentence.

Freedom for Ray was still deferred.

3

OPTIMISM AND PRAGMATISM

In Ray Bishop's refrain of 'I'm a good person, I'm a good person' can be heard echoes of a famous self-help tract approaching its centenary. The brainchild of an apothecary from the small French town of Troyes, *Self-Mastery through Conscious Autosuggestion* (1922) unleashed upon the world what became known and widely followed as the Coué Method.

Advocating twice-daily repetitions of a simple mantra, Emile Coué stripped the idea of authoring one's own life right down to the basics. He argued that the 'implanting of an idea in oneself by oneself' could harness the power of the imagination to astonishing effect, yielding near-miraculous change across an extraordinary spectrum of ailments and ills, both physical and psychological. The mantra itself may ring some bells, widely referenced as it is from Graham Greene to P. G. Wodehouse, John Lennon to the Pink Panther:

Tous les jours à tous points de vue je vais de mieux en mieux.
Every day in every way I'm getting better and better.

Repeat these words of unblemished optimism – this desire for change – like a dose of good medicine, twenty times or more, both morning and evening, and they would, promised Monsieur Coué, bring 'physical health to the sick [and] moral health to the neurotic and the erring'. As if by magic (or metamorphosis), here was a way to turn the crux of why we want to change into the *how*.

With a little unblemished optimism of his own, Coué added a section to his thesis subtitled 'The Superiority of This Method', asserting that 'by following my advice, it is impossible to fail'. He set about listing sundry cases from the Troyes countryside thus happily resolved: 'Little M-' cured, at a stroke, of both bed-wetting and kleptomania, 'Mlle. D-' delivered of her asthma in eight days flat, 'Mme. Z-' relieved of constipation and 'Mme F-' of sore knees, while lucky 'M. Y-' was apparently restored from suicidal depression to happiness in little more than a month.

There were sceptics, of course. Contemporary reporters went ferreting after evidence to suggest that such positive effects were at best temporary, while from the ascendant psychoanalytical camp came howls of lofty dissent. Yet, however crude Coué's methods – or his 'trick', as he once let slip – indeed however shaky his claims, the reason his mantra so resonated with people all over the world and for so long lies in its beguiling combination of unassailable optimism and intuitive faith in the power of self-belief.

Modern psychology has refined and re-branded that power as 'self-efficacy', a term coined and systematised in the late 1970s into a 'Unifying Theory of Behaviour Change' by one of the great psychologists of the twentieth century, Albert Bandura. Distinct from self-confidence or self-esteem – and optimistic in flavour, if not in essence – the notion of 'self-efficacy' specifically homes in on our belief in the capability of our own agency, our faith, whether well founded or otherwise, in our ability to achieve certain goals. High but not overweening self-efficacy is, on the whole, a plus for anyone wanting to get something done; nearly four decades of experimentation have proved time and again the positive effects it can have on aspiration, choice, motivation and upon action itself. And if change is the task in hand, then a belief in your ability to change turns out to be a key predictor of whether you actually can.

So that chipper mantra of Emile Coué, although not by a long chalk the optimal way to build self-efficacy, nor much of a tonic for constipation or sore knees either, stands as testament to the fact that the apothecary of Troyes was nevertheless barking up the right tree. For the desire for change does require both some shred of optimism and a glimmer of belief that such optimism may be borne out before any of us can be mobilised for action.

At the end of the summer of 2014 the Chinese National People's Congress Standing Committee unveiled proposals for the extension of democracy in Hong Kong in 2017. On the table was something that resembled the long-fought-for universal suffrage – one person, one vote – but there was a catch. Yes, the people of the Special Administrative Region would be invited for the first time to vote for their chief executive, but it turned out that the pool of candidates on offer would be selected by a small pro-Beijing nominating committee. It was to be Democracy Lite and anger in Hong Kong flared.

In the weeks that followed, extraordinary scenes unfolded. Amid glossy towers and elevated walkways that siphon moneyed shoppers from one mall to another, tens of thousands of people took to the streets to protest at what they saw as Beijing's failure to offer them free and fair elections.

Although vocal, the huge crowd was peaceful, armed only with placards and a myriad of coloured umbrellas, like 'a flexible rainbow', as one local man put it, first against the rain, then against the police use of pepper spray in an attempt to disperse the throng and finally primarily yellow umbrellas, the colour long associated with suffrage movements, as Hong Kong's own symbol of peaceful defiance.

The thing that surprised everyone, from party head-quarters in Beijing to campaigners on the island itself, not to mention commentators around the globe, was that the multitude simply refused to go home. The city ground to a halt. What had begun primarily as a student protest pulled in ordinary people from all over Hong Kong. They pitched tents, they opened noodle kitchens and study areas and simply remained on the streets, some of them for many weeks.

To the outside world all this looked, if not exactly like optimism – there were too many police in riot gear, too much tear gas and pepper spray for that – then certainly like collective efficacy on an epic scale. Here was a mass desire for change expressed in an essentially hopeful gesture of belief in its possibility by the weak against the strong, the yellow umbrella against the black baton and the gun. Indeed, Albert Bandura himself argues that this kind of communal belief in the power of human agency is not simply the sum of the self-efficacy of each individual participant. No, it is a new potency in and of itself, one that is inherently collective. But how does that appetite for wider social change relate to the individual, each man or woman in that crowd? Why does the micro become the macro?

A month or two after the protests died down, with no tangible concession from Beijing, the chairperson of the pro-democracy Democratic Party and long-time thorn in the side of the Chinese government, Emily Lau, sits in her office at the Hong Kong Legislative Council. If the region has one figure who has both weathered the convulsive change to have shaken Hong Kong over the last half-century and also tried to drive that change, then it is Emily. It is not that she has changed much herself – she says this – but seeking change around her is Emily's *raison d'être*.

Perched at a desk heaped high with papers, a laser print of *Je Suis Charlie* blu-tacked to the wall behind her, alongside the 'Umbrella Revolution' cover of *Time* magazine, Emily is small but formidable. She is wearing, one imagines not by accident, an extraordinary tailored Puffa jacket of the brightest yellow, the colour of the protests, and she takes from a drawer a yellow leather ribbon in a cellophane packet that reads 'Love' and 'Peace'. It reminds one of Ray Bishop's 'freedom' tattoo – but Emily's is a very different kind of freedom from that.

'We knew the protests had to come to an end', she says, looking at the ribbon in the packet and then handing it over like a calling card. 'The people staying there on the streets for so long, of course, very good, very brave. But that is wrong' – she flicks a thumb back irritably at the *Time* magazine cover – 'it's not a revolution. They don't want to overthrow the government. It's a movement for universal suffrage, very peaceful, but they would not budge. So what do you do to remove them? Tear gas? It didn't work. Are you going to use water cannons? Are you going to send the People's Liberation Army out on them? Tanks? Tiananmen Square?'

Emily does not mind being provocative. It is what she

does. But her point is strategic. A revolution can fail; a movement goes on. It is about why we want to change as much as it is about how to do it.

'Anyway I'm sure we will get change', she says briskly, plumping one of the piles on the desk and popping her smartphone on top of it.

'Are you?'

'Yes, but I don't know when. I possibly won't see democracy in Hong Kong in my lifetime' – just shy of her sixty-third birthday, Emily glances out of the window at the soupy wash of the bay and the towers of Kowloon beyond – 'change maybe, but we're talking about the ultimate: full democracy and democracy anywhere is the result of struggle and sacrifices by people over the generations, so – '.

Her phone vibrates.

'Can you give me one minute?' she says, 'I've got reporters asking me about a press conference tonight. I just WhatsApp them' – typing furiously with two thumbs – 'This WhatsApp is very useful.'

After studying in America and a spell in London first at the LSE and later with the BBC, Emily Lau returned to Hong Kong for good in 1984, the year of the Joint Declaration between Britain and China on the future of the British colony. A few years later she quit her job as a journalist and went into politics full-time. Over the almost quarter of a century that has followed, through the handover and beyond, Lau has devoted herself to the cause of democracy here, first in extended wrangles with the British and now with Beijing. As she says, in that boisterously chatty way she has of discussing all things, 'Oh, I despise both the British and the Chinese for the way they have treated us. Do you want a tea? A water?'

Emily has finished WhatsApping the reporters. 'And you were saying?' she says, pressing 'Send' with a flourish.

'Do you ever get personally weary of the struggle?'

'Well, it's just that I am very determined, I don't give up. I think it's just in my character. Like a bad penny, I keep turning up' and she hoots with laughter. 'What makes Emily tick is a question that has been asked me at least two hundred times and I always say the same thing.' She leans forward and glares theatrically. 'I don't want anybody to walk all over me. I will not be cowed. I just fight back. And when I see something unjust, I don't care who you are, I will speak out.'

From a story of political fundraising with a loudhailer and a cardboard box on a street corner in Causeway Bay – 'I collected over 160,000 Hong Kong dollars [more than US$20,000] in six or seven hours' – to the time she took the Chinese government to court and lost over a personal data breach – 'They went berserk!' – Emily Lau is a model of tenacity. It is a quality she says she inherited from her mother, a tiny woman who could neither read nor write but who was given to yelling at any official who got in her way with a ferocity Emily recalls with clear affection. This, then, is one example of the micro level of that mass desire for change, a very personal need for autonomy. Through Hong Kong's years of upheaval any attempts to intimidate Lau – excrement hung from her office door and a twenty-year ban on visiting the Chinese mainland, as well as long-term surveillance – seem to have done little to disturb her *modus operandi*. She does not, she says, feel in any personal danger, 'not yet'. And therein may lie her reputation for being resolute to the point of mulishness. It is not for nothing that the last governor of Hong Kong, Chris Patten, dubbed Emily 'the headbanger'.

Reminded of this, she lets out a little yelp of exasperation, even though it was nearly twenty years ago. 'Because he thinks that I kept concentrating on things which are impossible. He had this "drop of democracy" proposal' – she rolls her eyes – 'and he said "Why don't you take that? You want full democracy, but that's not possible and still you keep banging your head against this brick wall, so why bang it? Why go for something impossible?" But that's what I've been doing for decades' – Emily smiles and pats her black hair – 'and my head is still intact, more or less. I may give this impression that I'm unbending, unyielding, banging, but in fact if you look at my track record in the council I am a very pragmatic person. I always say that politics is the art of the possible, I understand you need to compromise to get things done. But there are limits and over certain crucial things, human rights, democracy, I will not compromise.' These last four words she beats out with a small fist on the desk.

In 1959 a maverick sociology professor at Columbia University in New York came up with an idea as refreshingly unorthodox as he was. A bulky Texan with a great love of motor bikes and a disinclination to dress in the sober flannels of his academic peers, Charles Wright Mills stood out like a sore thumb in the hushed precincts of Ivy League academe. Yet in spite of that – or perhaps because of it – he carved out a new way of thinking about why we want change that would become a pillar of twentieth-century sociology.

C. Wright Mills's big idea grew from his ferocious critique of the trend in social science to regard the individual and society as entirely separate concepts. Instead, Mills argued that we should endeavour to understand the lines of connection between the two, the micro and the macro, the 'private troubles' of an individual's everyday life and the 'public issues' of society at large. The heart of his idea was that the large-scale tectonics of social history are intimately entwined with the sentiments and small decisions of the personal experience. It was a 'vivid awareness' of these connections that Mills dubbed 'the sociological imagination'. In its way it offers the flip side to that unified view of why people want change, the one exemplified immaculately by Shelley's great anthem to people power, *The Masque of Anarchy*:

Rise like lions after slumber
In unvanquishable number!
Shake your chains to earth like dew
Which in sleep had fallen on you:
Ye are many – they are few!

Yet Mills's point was that in every change movement there is also a less homogeneous, less lionish side to the story. And that is how it was beneath those yellow umbrellas in Hong Kong in 2014. The streets of the city, over those seventy-nine days, flowed not with a single cohesive movement but with a large, diverse group of individuals and a host of 'private troubles' which coalesced in that moment around the grand 'public issue' of democratic representation.

Above all, attempting to humanise what had become an increasingly theoretical discipline, Wright, like Emile Coué, albeit for very different reasons, put the human imagination and our desire for autonomy at the centre of his thinking. Why we want to change the world is not, after all, so very different from why we want to change in smaller ways too. And if we can only teach ourselves to think that way, then there is every cause for optimism.

Emily Lau gets a bit tetchy if you ask her loose theoretical questions about change – what it is, what it means, what it feels like. She just stonewalls them, returning to the pragmatic core arguments she has spent a lifetime making. She clearly does not wish to theorise; she wants to get things done. That is why she is in politics.

'Look, I've had two marriages and two divorces,' she says, shuffling a handful of papers from one pile to another, 'and I remember a friend of mine said to me, he said, "Emily, you are married to your work."' She raises her eyebrows. 'Because actually for many, many years, I spent a lot of time here in the legislative council and that's what I wanted to do and if' – she swallows – '*people* cannot accept it, then they say "OK, goodbye". And I say "OK, goodbye". So this is the thing: I'm not actually married to my work, but I'm married to the good of Hong Kong and because of that, all other family things play second fiddle.'

The English word 'umbrella' is derived from the Latin *umbella*, denoting the protective petals of the umbel flower, but in Cantonese the same word, 遮, *ze*, is used both for the handy rain-shield and for the verb 'to block or obstruct'. It reads like a metaphor both for Emily's life and for the change movement with which she is now associated.

'Belief in the possibility of change is very important', she says, glancing out of the window towards Tim Mei Avenue, where the last few tents festooned with wind-chimes and yellow ribbons are still pitched. 'Because it means hope and, especially if you're a politician, you have to give the people hope. Protesting is fine, but if all they see is complete darkness, pessimism, no hope, no change, they're not going to work with you. And you have to work with other people because you cannot create change single-handedly. But it is also important for politicians and others, not to always be so very optimistic either –'.

'Are you not an optimist?'

'No,' says Emily, firmly.

'Aren't you?'

She shakes her head.

'I am a realist. I remember after the change of sovereignty in '97,' she says, 'and a foreign diplomat he said to me "Now, Miss Lau, can you tell me why you are so unremittingly pessimistic?" and I said that I'm not an optimist, because there isn't much reason to be optimistic.'

She growls this line and then snaps, 'But' – tapping the desk as though to get one's full attention – 'I am very positive and I'm always working to achieve democracy. I can't say it's going to happen next year or the year after that and I won't deceive people. But nor will I say that what you want will never happen. So I say we've got to fight hard and then maybe, *maybe* it will.'

She stands and picks up a sheaf of papers for her next meeting. 'You know, I think if we all work together, it will happen.' And that, for today, is all Emily Lau has to say on the matter.

4

A GOOD DAY AT
THE OFFICE

'All that matters', Sigmund Freud once said, 'is love and work.' We shall come to the heart erelong, but anyone who finds themselves deleting junk email from people with improbable names and with subject lines like *What Is Your Dream Job?* or *The Best Careers Advice You'll Ever Get!* will know that these only make good spam because the world of work is such a universal source of discontent. *Hey! Aren't you fatigued? Making less cash than you want?* Er, yes, Mr Spam, but the point is a serious one: our working lives, as we have seen with Ed Coxon, are a wellspring of change desires.

Figures from a recent Gallup poll of 1.4 million employees worldwide reveal a crisis of happiness in the workplace. According to the research, only a tiny 13 per cent of the workforce across 142 countries are deemed to be 'engaged'; 63 per cent are 'not engaged', 'sleepwalking through their workday, putting time but not energy or passion into their work'; and 24 per cent are 'actively disengaged' – that is to say, 'not just unhappy at work but busy acting out their unhappiness'. For anyone pondering why we want to change, this equates to an epidemic of longing for things to be different.

What grabs headlines, of course, is that all this dissatisfaction costs the global economy dear. The Gallup figures go on to enumerate the stark differences in performance between the happy workers and the unhappy to a toll that amounts to many hundreds of billions of dollars every year.

Into this fray stalks Colin Price with a mandate to lessen that price-tag. Tall, grey and a little lanky, he is dressed today in dark blue from head to toe, the crown of an expensive wrist-watch peeping out of a soft knitted cuff the colour of a night sky. Gurus are not typically called Colin, but this one is. One of the foremost consultants working in his field, Colin Price is a change guru, not that he would ever call himself such. He is too pragmatic for that. Yet Colin has a formidable reputation for getting large groups within a workforce to figure out what they want to change, what they *need* to change and then helping them to change it. On paper, his might seem largely an external project perhaps not so different from that of Emily Lau, albeit minus the political conscience – but that would be wrong on both counts. For there is more conscience in Colin's work than one might imagine and it is all about changing minds and behaviours right down at micro level.

'The thing that pisses me off', he says, removing a bottle of mineral water from a large shiny fridge filled with such bottles and placing it unopened on the thick glass table, 'is when I get treated like an estate agent. No offence to estate agents, but I get really tense if someone behaves in a way that says "Well, you're just here to make the money." Yes, they are paying you a lot of money, but it upsets me because really I think of myself as a corporate doctor. I'm there to make things healthy, but people's mental image of a consultant is a clipboard and a calculator, which couldn't be further from the truth. So yes, woe is me,' and he laughs, sweeping an invisible crumb from the spotless table-top, 'but my work is who I am and it's hugely important to me. I'm just consumed by this idea that it would be better if the world was a happier place, so I'm sad when people are in that *Death of a Salesman* mode, every day is the same, no volition. That's not a great life to have, is it?'

Colin Price has spent thirty years as a management consultant in the City of London, fifteen of them as a director at McKinsey, and recently his own boutique consultancy was acquired by Heidrick & Struggles, a global human capital giant. It is a line of work not usually noted for its idealism. The only umbrellas here are for rainy days. But it is one into which Colin says he 'stumbled' via his political convictions. As a student, he was passionately preoccupied with the neo-Marxist economics of labour versus capital, a militancy that over time gave way to an idea that perhaps one could bring about change for ordinary people not by fighting capitalism but by working from within.

'I remember when I was a student,' he says, 'one of my professors played a scene from *I Love Lucy* where Desi Arnaz says to Lucille Ball "Can't you just be happy?" and she says to him "There's more to life than happiness" and that's the punchline, because of course there is nothing more to life than happiness.' Colin looks out of a high Regency window at the sun-dappled leaves of a sapling outside. 'It just stuck with me for years and years, that. And so I discovered what I thought was an appropriate nexus between my politics and earning a living and that was making organisations work better and become more human, happier, at the same time.'

That early idea of happiness found practical iteration in what Colin, in corporate doctor mode, now prefers to call 'organisational health'. He describes how, when he started out in this work, there were no diagnostic tools for measuring the working culture of organisations; indeed there was little idea of there being such a thing as 'culture' at all. But Colin and others have changed that via empirical proof that 'good health' – a happy, engaged workforce who know what they are meant to be doing and are given both the means and the encouragement to do it – is proven to generate 'better outcomes', as Colin calls them. He counts these outcomes on two long, knuckly fingers: 'both more money and a richer experience of your life'. Then he adds, 'So the soft stuff dramatically impacts the hard stuff. There's a synthesis between economic reality and our experience of the world. And the work that I'm proud of, after all these years, is that "Who We Are" work, but you don't get to play with the "Who We Are" unless you can stick some money on the bottom line.'

That corporate *realpolitik* is what Colin Price has become highly skilled at navigating and this is where change comes in. For however up to date their shiny, business self-help books, however noisy the professed concern for the well-being of their workforce, in reality, senior executives only call in consultants like Colin when there is what might politely be termed a 'performance trigger' – or, as Colin puts it, an 'Oh shit' moment when they realise that things are going wrong. Driven by a pressure for greater transparency in big business and a rapidity in the capital markets, the average tenure of a CEO has dropped from around twenty years in the early 1980s to just six years today, and so those 'Oh shit' moments come around with increasing regularity. This is why – as Colin says, 'Bang!' – the demand for corporate change programmes has in recent years grown exponentially.

It may be appropriate at this point to recollect that the etymology of the word 'change' has itself taken a turn or two about the market-place. Believed to be derived from the Proto-Indo-European root *kemb-*, meaning 'to bend' or 'to crook', the word proved its own ability to turn a corner by next cropping up in Latin with a distinctly mercantile purpose. Meaning to exchange or to barter, the classical Latin *cambire* then morphed into the vernacular *cambiare*, at which point it seems to have added to its commercial function a more generic idea of exchange. From there the word travelled on, as subject to the restlessness of linguistic flux as any other. Still echoing with the market-place cries of buy and sell, it next materialises in the Old French *changier*, 'to swap' or 'switch'. It was not until the thirteenth century that 'change' finally appeared in English and over the centuries that followed, it gradually shed some, but never quite all, of its connotations of transaction. In the 1400s we began to change our clothes, a century or so later our minds. Tunes and hearts followed, but, even in the modern usage of 'change', you can still hear the jingle of coins and the sound of haggling.

In the interests of discretion, Colin Price's corporate change clients cannot be listed here, but rest assured, the line-up bristles with household names from across big business, the financial sector and public services. While the idea is not altogether comforting that these organisations, so central in our society, seem to find themselves in one pickle after another, it is nevertheless soothing to know that Colin is on the case. After an hour or two in his company, you feel that he might do a rather good job of sorting out your life too. And that is because, again and again, Colin Price comes up with arresting insights – on why we want to change and how that desire can be harnessed – that seem to reach far beyond the bounds of business.

One such is his wry view of a certain form of catastrophism that can overtake people entertaining a change. This manifests itself in organisations as a widespread tendency for bosses to cast some modest adaptation to an existing paradigm as – Colin booms – 'A Fundamental Cultural Transformation!' He laughs a lot at this and then goes on to describe the flip side: 'But there are times when the very thing that formed your strength in the old model would be unhelpful to the new model. That is real transformation. Think of the butterfly and the caterpillar and the cocoon. So the very thing that rooted you to the tree is not the thing that's going to help you to fly.'

This leads Colin to reject the oft-peddled view that most workforces are fundamentally psychologically resistant to large-scale change. According to him, they simply are not. What they are resistant to, and fearful of, he says, is loss. This is Colin's intuitive take on a well-known cognitive bias, identified in 1984 by the psychologists Daniel Kahneman and Amos Tversky and known as 'loss aversion', which demonstrates how losses loom larger in our minds than gains of equal size. Colin's point, one of several side-swipes he makes at executive arrogance, is that reading this fear of loss as a resistance to change often amounts to – and he acts it out – 'Obviously what I'm doing is right and I have a problem in managing the plebs, so will you please help me to better manipulate them.' He makes a little grunt of disgust and adds, 'actually the opposite is true, which is the audience out there are looking at the change you want to make and they're working out *Is it going to be good for me, or is it going to be bad for me?* And if they see what you've got as *good for me*, they're not resistant to it at all.'

That, says Colin, is why anyone wishing to pursue a change needs a story that is attractive and exciting to the people whose lives will be affected and one that does more than simply set fire to the past or the present. In an echo of Ray Bishop's story, Colin says that simply showing people a 'burning platform', although all too common, is a lousy way of motivating them to change. Instead you must offer them the 'shining beacon' of a hopeful future and that can be conjured with structured, imaginative effort. Ask yourself, he says, five key questions about why we want to change:

1. (Honestly) where are we now?
2. Where do I (realistically) believe we should be?
3. What's the risk of where we might get to?
4. What can we imagine as the first five steps?
5. Why does it matter?

Weave these into a credible and appealing script and you have taken the reins, all but setting the stage for the 'how': the change itself.

Any reader weighing up a change in his or her own life might choose this moment to go and fetch a pencil and paper, because there is more of this pragmatic wisdom on the way. As Colin shifts on his chair, now leaning in to draw an imaginary diagram on the table, now getting up and pacing to tease out an idea, some of what he says is clothed in the patois of business-speak. Yet there remains a powerful sense here of a lifetime's experience of helping humdrum, everyday people to change the way they work. Managing their tics and neuroses, their egotism and their mistakes, he dignifies their underlying desire to feel good about what they do for a living. As Colin says, 'You don't have to like your clients, but it is essential to love them. You've got to see beyond the bad behaviour, because there's a lot of that, into the human being behind it. And that behaviour is actually just a trigger into an opportunity to change the world for the better.' Colin talks a lot about changing the world and gradually you realise that what he is really talking about is changing people, offering them a new kind of autonomy, bartering some of their bad days for good ones.

Colin Price is now busy discussing what he calls 'the most important issue of all': the speed with which the leadership of an organisation cracks on with the change process itself. This is, he says, measurably and substantially more influential on increased performance than anything else – there is a lesson for us all in that – but then something fascinating and rather extraordinary happens.

Colin Price has devoted nearly two hours now to the desire for change, the need for change, the why, the what, the when, but when asked about the how, the mystery of what actually brings the change about, he says this: 'OK, there's a list of thirty things we know work – training, hiring new people, building hero teams, telling stories, high use of consequences, etcetera etcetera, so we know these work' – and then Colin pauses for a long time – 'but here's the big thing we don't know. *We don't know which of them works.* Haven't got the foggiest as to whether intervention no. 13, was it great? Good? Average? Poor? Terrible? We have no way of measuring that. So in this field, the shift over the last fifty years has been that culture matters and we can measure it. The shift over the next fifty needs to be "This is how you architect change. This is the combination of interventions, the weaving of them, that makes a difference, because at the moment we're in the absolute foothills of our understanding about that.'"

There is another pause.

'So how do you do it?'

'Shall I tell you the honest truth?' he says. 'I sit down with a bit of paper and I go *I think it's this*' – he grins, almost as though he is glad to get this off his chest – 'and I often smile to myself, because when I then write what we should do, often it takes five years to do those things and costs hundreds of millions, sometimes billions of pounds. But it all comes from that piece of paper and, yes, it is somewhat intuitive.' He shrugs.

'Does that give you a sense of power?'

'Yeah', he says and as he laughs out loud, it is hard to tell whether Colin is joking or not.

This conversation about the mechanics and the mysteries of why we want to change has unfolded in a setting of considerable splendour: a fine Regency villa of golden stone in the city of Bath, with a lavish, hyper-modern interior, all sleek lines in bold colours, large abstract modern paintings and artfully placed *objets* dotted here and there. Colin mentions that this is just one of three homes, a 'big house' in France, another in Cornwall 'and we're buying a place in London as well,' he says, 'so one of the changes that's happened in my life is that I've become wealthy as a result of this work, but look, treat this in the way it's intended.'

And only now at the very end does it become clear quite the scale of Colin Price's own personal transformation, the extent of his metamorphosis. He mentions, as though he is not sure that it is either interesting or relevant, that he was born in Shettleston, one of the most deprived neighbourhoods in Glasgow, where his family lived in a tenement flat with no bathroom. 'We'd go to the swimming baths to have a wash', he says. When his father could not find work, the family moved south to Preston and from there it was 'rough school, council estate, lots of bad behaviour, failed my 11-plus' – Colin smiles – 'so that image that one has of a predictive life, an I-went-to-Eton-Goldman-Sachs type life: I'm the exact opposite of that and then I end up' – he pauses for a moment – 'well, in a very different kind of world. Maybe that's why I say people don't fear change, they fear loss, because that to me is a positive change. I didn't fear it in any way.' And he leans back in his chair and looks around the room.

5

ON SURVIVAL

This man is also sitting, but not on an elegant, transparent acrylic chair. It is early April 1994 and we are in a small mud-floored house in a village in southern Rwanda. The man has a spear in one hand, a machete in the other. It has been a busy morning and he is taking the weight off his feet by resting on an upturned *umuvure*, a wooden canoe-shaped vessel used for squashing fermented bananas with sorghum to make *urwagwa*, banana beer.

Here begins another very different tale of mobility, a resounding rejection of the predictive life for sure, but one so extraordinary in its darkness and its light that it should sound a clarion call to anyone doubtful of how powerful a desire for change can become.

'So where are they,' the man says, almost casually, 'Apolinnaire's family?'

Another man, also carrying a machete and spear, is pacing and looking about the room with its low bed and wooden ply walls. 'We don't have any record that they've been killed', he says. 'They must be somewhere.' And he shoots a glance out through an unglazed window into the shimmering heat.

This is not the first time these men have been here in the last few days and the Hutu owner of this humble dwelling, Félix, mutely shakes his head.

'Come on!' barks the man sitting on the *umuvure*. 'You must know where Kaguru is! And his family.'

Kaguru is Apolinnaire's nickname about the village. It means 'leg' and it is what he has long been called by less kindly neighbours because of a pronounced limp he has had since childhood.

'I don't', Félix says. 'I don't know where they are.'

But Félix does know. Apolinnaire, his dear old friend, is a Tutsi and is hiding in a ditch just outside the window where Félix ripens bananas for beer under a thick covering of palm branches. Under the *umuvure* on which the man with the spear and the machete is sitting, looking at the soles of his shoes through a thin crack of light: Apolinnaire's two little sons, Protais, aged ten, and Hyppolite, just seven.

More questions, more denials, more threats and eventually the men leave, but they will be back. A little trickle of pee seeps out from underneath the *umuvure*.

The boys, Félix's godsons, have spent several days here. At night, they sleep under Félix and his wife's bed. Apolinnaire stays in the ditch, disguised as fermenting bananas, but his sons visit him there for a few minutes every dinnertime when it is dark. They listen to the grown-ups talking with their father about who has been killed, which families and where, how they were flushed out of their hiding places. Nobody eats much.

The tension has been simmering for months, Apolinnaire beaten up on the road home from the rice fields, crops stolen without recourse from his family's tiny plot by their grass-roofed hut. Then on the radio, news that the president's plane had crashed and the shock-wave that followed. Within twenty-four hours they were packing their few belongings, burying what they could not carry in the banana plantation next door, scrambling into all the clothes they owned and running for their lives, the boys and their father in one direction towards Félix's house, their mother and elder sisters in the other. And around them the killing began.

Now nearly a week into the bloodshed, the seven-day fermentation period for the ditch of bananas is up, so Apolinnaire must make the dangerous trek at night to the large Catholic missionary church at Mibirizi, where many Tutsis have taken refuge. The boys stay under the bed or the *umuvure* for a few days more, but the men come back and back. Outside, the situation is escalating; soon even children are no safer than their parents. So on a Sunday morning Félix's wife takes Hyppolite and Protais by the hand, as though they are her own Hutu children, and they walk as a family to church, little knowing what will unfold there tomorrow.

Hyppolite Ntigurirwa is now twenty-nine. He tells this story, sitting on a classroom chair in a large, empty seminar room that smells of new plastic and whiteboard markers. The university is quiet for the holidays and slate-grey blinds are pulled down against the watery English sunshine outside, a single strip light aglow above the door. Dressed in mossy green and beige from shirt to shoes, his smooth dark face open, direct and animated, Hyppolite seems like a little shred of quick, organic matter in this anodyne modern box. His hands map apocalyptic scenes on the melamine table-top and even when speaking of terrible things, he smiles, as though somehow not wishing to bruise the listener with his story.

He tells how, now reunited with their father at Mibirizi Parish Church and in a large crowd of many hundreds of local Tutsis, he and his brother felt safe at first. The following morning Protais made an excursion back to the village to fetch food, but within hours at the church all hell broke loose. First mortars were fired at the building. Then what Hyppolite calls 'the killers' came in and started calling out names.

'And they started' – he pauses, smiles – 'and they started and they started. Killing.'

Apolinnaire grabbed Hyppolite's hand. They fled into the church grounds, Hyppolite hiding in one dark, thick bush and his father in another a few metres away. Two or three hours passed.

'We could hear everything,' he says. 'People hunting and killing. Just that, for hours.' He holds a steady gaze.

Then Apolinnaire, who had caught a cold hiding in the banana ditch, made a fatal mistake: he coughed.

'It was like hunters finding an animal', says Hyppolite. 'They just said, "Oh, here's a Tutsi. It's a cockroach – come!" They were passing by where I was and I thought maybe it's me, so I was waiting and thinking how am I going to die? Because I knew that I was to die. But then they went and they killed my –'. He clears his throat. 'I knew they were killing him, but I couldn't do anything. I can remember the noise of my father being killed, the last sound that he made.'

Hyppolite is quiet for a moment. Then he tells how over several hours the killing gradually slowed and stopped. An awful silence fell. The seven-year-old emerged from the bush and, in the fading light, walked over to where his father had been.

'I don't even know why I was going there, but I did. And

when I looked at where he'd been hiding, I saw – ' Hyppolite draws a line on the table-top with his finger – 'dogs. Dogs were eating the body of my dad.' There is a long pause. 'Even today, when I think of it, I don't know what to say. I'd seen some dead people on the way to the church, but now I saw many, many people all around me' – Hyppolite blows out a measured breath – 'like bodies were the leaves of plants'. He looks up and he smiles again.

At dawn Hyppolite returned to the village. He found his brother and together they spent the next two weeks hiding by day at their godfather's house, by night, when the search for surviving Tutsis was now at its most intense, in the burned-out ruins of their home or in the undergrowth of the banana plantation. There, through a lattice of foliage, they witnessed another massacre of local Tutsis late one night, their cousins and many friends among them, but somehow – 'we don't really know how or why', he says – Hyppolite and Protais survived.

A month after the massacre at the church, Hyppolite and his brother found their way to a UNHCR refugee camp in Nyarushishi and there they were reunited with two of their sisters. When it was announced at the end of that year that it was safe to return home, they did and joined their mother, who had come out of hiding. Their home in ruins, the family lived for a while at a nearby RPF (Rwandan Patriotic Front) soldiers' camp.

From the camp, little Hyppolite started school and it was in that moment that his life began to turn. For what makes this harrowing testimony a powerful story of change is down to what happened next to Hyppolite Ntigurirwa.

Some eight years before the genocide in Rwanda, two

American psychologists, Hazel Markus and Paula Nurius, published a now famous paper in which they posited a new way of thinking about the bounds and the workings of who we are. Entitled *Possible Selves*, the paper's central proposition was simple but revolutionary: that a significant yet often overlooked part of us lies not in the present but in the future. We are not simply who we feel ourselves to be today, but also the people we imagine we could become tomorrow.

These imagined future selves, the psychologists argued, have a number of important and somewhat counter-intuitive features. First, they are not necessarily anchored in reality, some cool-headed calculation on the basis of today's facts of what tomorrow is likely to bring. Nor do these possible selves always represent the best-case scenario. Instead, alongside any dream we might harbour of our ideal self, the happy, wealthy, attractive, successful version, there are also other possible selves, those that surrender to what we feel is attainable and also those that plunge deep into our darkest fears of loneliness, failure, poverty, rejection. Perhaps the most important feature of this gaggle of possible selves is that they do not travel alone, but rather that any of us, at any given time, has a number of possible selves that jostle and barge like a crowd of schoolchildren, according to the conditions of the present.

This combination of unruly plurality, the essential unpredictability of the future and a tendency to play fast and loose with the present facts is, Markus and Nurius argued, the reason why these possible selves had spent so long in the wilderness of psychological study. In general, the science always sought to drill down towards some core, the most true, the most central, the most authentic. Little heed was paid to what Markus and Nurius characterised as 'a continually active, shifting array of available self-knowledge', its distortions, its wild flights of imaginative fancy or fear. In so doing, contended the paper, we had all but ignored the very architecture of our lives over time, the way in which we concoct, achieve or resist a restless throng of possible selves.

Their point was that this inner realm of make-believe is more than imaginative background noise. It can and does direct not only our hopes and fears, but also more practical aspects of motivation and behaviour, serving to form what Markus and Nurius call 'cognitive bridges between the present and future'. In this way, these possible selves, the fruit of our ever-stirring imagination, turn out to be the building blocks of the new stories we write for ourselves. They are the very fount of change and sometimes even redemption.

Between 800,000 and a million Rwandans died in just a hundred days of genocide in 1994, 2,000 of them at Mibirizi Parish, and the world failed to stop it. What that says about human agency would seem to be bleak indeed, small reason to believe in one young man's ability to make a new world for himself. But Hyppolite Ntigurirwa is a survivor. Indeed the word 'survivor' is one he wears with dignity, even with pride. It is both who he is and who he will be, a possible self that has in turn powered an astonishing transformation.

Think back to that idea of a 'predictive life', the possible self that would say Ed Coxon was not 'cut out' to be a police officer, nor Ray Bishop a good man, nor Colin Price a wealthy City slicker, and then ponder, if you will, what that deterministic model would dictate for a child like Hyppolite. If you are raised in a grass-roofed hut – 'hut' is Hyppolite's word – to an impoverished family and then you are submitted to wholesale carnage and trauma before you are even ten, what then have you been 'cut out' to be? A broken man or a brutal one? An addict? A suicide?

This is a question that Hyppolite Ntigurirwa has often, he says, asked himself. He dreads to think 'what kind of person I could be today' and he counts those possible selves on his fingers: drug-addicted, drunk, violent, vengeful; 'maybe a soldier, a very bad soldier', he adds. 'This is what happened to many orphans of genocide who didn't go to school and maybe if I hadn't, I would be like them. So I would say I was lucky.' For what saved Hyppolite – of this he is adamant – was both an awareness of these dire options, drummed into him by his mother, and the conjuring of another imagined self, redeemed and transformed through education.

After the genocide, little by little, the family rebuilt their home and their lives. The wounds were still fresh, but when Hyppolite was at school – his mother always made him go – he felt happy and he soon found himself at the top of the class.

Surfing a wave of high marks, Hyppolite went on to high school, then into teacher-training and eventually to the University of Rwanda in Butare. His fees were paid by the Survivors Fund, a fact that sometimes caused resentment among the other students, but which fed Hyppolite's appetite to understand what had happened to him 'and who I am', he says with a fervour that suggests the process is still under way. The funding also made him work hard; the scholarships depended on it and so did the possible self through which Hyppolite now conjured a future as something other than a victim: Success, with a capital 'S'.

Success became Hyppolite's key driver. He was the first person from his family to go to high school, among the first from his village to go to university, and gradually the possibility of another kind of life began to open up for him, 'like', he says, 'you are going to get money and a good life and be a middle-class person', and he grins from ear to ear. On the purpose of education, Hyppolite is very clear. For him it is not some woolly notion of expanding the mind, some confection of intellectual edification. No, it stands for something real, 'a sense of life', as he puts it, and a means to an end.

'This education I was getting,' he says, 'it was saying to me everything can change. The courage that the teachers used to give me, they knew I was from a poor family but that if I learned all these things, that this was part of what makes people become successful. That if you do this, you will go and go and go' – Hyppolite gesticulates as though he is throwing his future self like a succession of balls into the far corner of the room – 'that was the real healing for me.'

One of the later writers in the school of the Greek physician Hippocrates put it like this: 'healing is a matter of time, but it is also sometimes a matter of opportunity.' Thus education gave Hyppolite Ntigurirwa both an opportunity for personal betterment and a way to take control of his life after the ravages of trauma. Not only that, but it also offered the possibility of another kind of change, another possible self.

During his second year of teacher-training, Hyppolite had been introduced to sociology. This had been a light-bulb moment, a chance to understand not just how people live together, but why and how they sometimes kill each other too. Sociology became his course of study at the University of Rwanda and a move to specialise thereafter in the sociology of conflict duly led him five and a half thousand miles away to this seminar room at Bristol University in England. Having watched lectures online by a professor here who specialises in multiculturalism, he had simply emailed him. This was not at all the done thing in the Rwandan educational hierarchy, but it was a gamble that paid off. A lengthy correspondence ensued and a year later Hyppolite is here on a full scholarship studying for a Masters.

It is an almost unimaginable leap for the little boy cowering under the *umuvure* that day back in April 1994. Or, as Hyppolite puts it, 'if there was a formula that said only the rich will remain rich and the poor will die poor, or that only people who have parents who went to school will go to school, then I wouldn't be here.' He taps the table-top with the outstretched fingers of both hands, going on to speak with great confidence about the complex problems of his homeland, about his hopes for the future there and for his part in it. All about him you can sense a veritable cavalcade of possible selves, hopes for a doctorate and a professorship perhaps, the many ideas for reconciliation projects in Rwanda that he likes to jot in the margins of his notebook. 'Maybe I will end up being a politician', he says and he laughs.

'If I think about the way I survived, what I went through,' he says, 'it trained me to think that there's only no hope when you die. I was almost dead, I saw people sitting on the vessel I was hiding in, looking for me to kill me. So sometimes there is only hope, nothing else. Anything can happen to me, in an optimistic way and also in a pessimistic way. That's why in my room here I've written myself a note and I read it every morning: I never fail until I fail. That's what my life's taught me and I think it works. I think I'm doing well, yeah.'

And he is. For in Hyppolite's story there meet so many reasons why we want to change and how we can. There is a past that, like Ray Bishop's, cannot be undone, but there is also redemption and hope for the future. There is growing up, as for Ed Coxon, but also a desire to change the world in which we live, as for both Emily Lau and Colin Price. There is an aspiration to happiness and a drive for self-determination, as each of these people has embodied, through engaging the power of the imagination with the possible selves of tomorrow. And yes, there is survival, having suffered the very worst that life can throw at you. It was Gandhi who famously said 'Be the change you want to see in the world' and that twin sense of being and wanting seems resonant with the very last thing Hyppolite said before he picked up his notebook and headed back to the university library. Asked if he forgave the people who had killed his father and cousins, he said this:

'Yes I do, but I didn't forgive them because it's easy, no. And I don't blame people who wouldn't forgive because I didn't immediately. It took me a while to think about why it happened as it did, why did they act like that, why? But if my place is to be about teaching people how to be kind, I couldn't do that if I didn't forgive. It's a very good technique of teaching if you forgive. And when I meet the people who killed members of my family, they live nearby my Mum, I say, "*Amakuru*." That's Kinyarwanda for "Hi" and I can see them think *How can you talk to us when we did what we did?* but that's what you can teach: even though you killed people, you can still be good. So I have forgiven, not because it's easy, but because I want to teach those people and others how we can make a good, a better world.'

PART II

HOW MUCH CAN WE CHANGE?

6

ON MAGIC TRICKS

Roll up! Roll up! Watch metamorphosis unfold before your very eyes!

For, on occasions, metamorphosis requires something of a conjuring trick in order to begin. In 1893 a young Hungarian-American magician and amateur stunt-artist called Ehrich Weiss appeared along with his younger brother Theodore at a side-show at Coney Island in New York. The climax of their act was a trick involving a second-hand substitution trunk. This was the first piece of magical apparatus that the nineteen-year-old tie-cutter from a neckwear factory on Broadway had saved up $25 to buy. The trick involved Ehrich, who went by the name of Ehrie or Harry, having his hands bound behind his back before being bundled into a large sack, which was then tied closed. Theodore would then heave the sack into a large box, which was strapped shut, locked and pulled inside the tall trunk, upon which a curtain was now drawn, obscuring both Theodore and his tightly parcelled brother. Three claps would resound from within. At the third, lo and behold, it would be Harry not Theodore who would triumphantly whip open the curtain and proceed to unstrap and unlock the box to reveal Theodore inside the sack, all knots secured as before. At this point, with any luck, the small crowd of day trippers would gasp, applaud and perhaps lob a dime or two onto the stage.

The double act was billed as The Houdini Brothers, a stage name (or possible self) the enterprising elder Weiss boy had cooked up after reading the memoirs of a famous French magician called Robert-Houdin. Their signature illusion, with its hidden doors and phoney knots, he dubbed Metamorphosis.

That summer at Coney Island the self-fashioned Harry Houdini also substituted a new wife for his brother. With the winsome Bess as his double-act partner, 'The Houdinis' now took the world by storm. At the heart of their act was Metamorphosis, the trick that would spark Houdini's own transformation into one of the greatest showmen in American history.

Of course, off stage and in the real world, change does not usually come about with an abracadabra and a few hooky knots. You cannot simply substitute yourself for another person or, with a clap of your hands, swap this imperfect world for a more reliable, just or peaceful one. Each of the people in this book knows that all too well.

Frequently this tough reality leads to the view that people do not really change, that they cannot really change, that we are imprisoned within our extant selves, body and mind, and that we had better lump it with what we have got. In some ways, of course, this is true. There are the things that we are stuck with: short legs, thin hair, a lopsided smile perhaps. Or in the case of personality, there are the so-called

'Big Five' basic character traits, as laid out by psychologists. There are the levels of neuroticism, extroversion, openness, agreeableness or conscientiousness that, according to some, remain stable and largely unchanged from late childhood onwards through life. Others in psychological science (Hazel Markus, of Possible Selves Theory, included) argue quite the reverse. They maintain that personality is supple, flexible and dynamic; that much of who we are occurs at levels between those broad traits and within our beliefs and behaviour, our sense of self and of agency. We should not forget the magnificent plasticity of our brains, or the cellular ephemerality of our bodies – and we shall come to those in due course – but when considering the extent to which any of us can really change, we would do well to keep in mind how far from clear consensus the experts on all this really are.

The reason may be because at some level *both camps are right*. This tension between what can and cannot change, between learning to accept our lot and fighting it, sits at the very heart of our lives. It is as the desperate Dr Jekyll confessed of the struggle with his infernal *doppelgänger*, Mr Hyde: 'I saw that of the two natures that contended in the field of my consciousness, even if I could rightly be said to be either, it was only because I was radically both.' Dr Jekyll's fevered point could also be said to hold for our relationship with change itself. In the struggle between our remarkable ability to transform in some ways and our abject inability to do so in others, if either is the reality, it is only because both are. You cannot change everything, but *you can change something*. And that leaves us with a slippery question indeed: not whether to try and change, or even why, but *what* – the heart, the mind, the senses, the body or even, perhaps, the name?

This question brings us to the whimsical parable of the two Alina Simones, a tale that has more than a little in common with Harry Houdini's Metamorphosis trick.

It is fitting that this story takes place in the City of Dreams, where, as the song says, 'these streets will make you feel brand new'. So take a walk up Broadway from Ehrie Weiss's old place of work at the tie factory, now the SoHo branch of Bloomingdale's. Stroll towards the raised lawns and market stalls of Union Square before ducking down a cross street into the enclave of Gramercy.

The woman sitting at her desk in an apartment on the twenty-second floor of a 1960s block there, her dark hair scraped loosely up and her glasses up on top of her head, is the first Alina Simone, the Original Alina Simone, if you like. A singer-songwriter of some repute with three widely acclaimed albums under her belt, she has not long passed her fortieth birthday, but the entity named Alina Simone is, she says, not yet fifteen years old.

Alina was born in Kharkov in the former Soviet Union, now in the eastern Ukraine. Her father, a physicist, was blacklisted by the KGB for non-cooperation and the family arrived in the USA as political refugees in 1976, when Alina was just one. She has, she says, no memory of life in the USSR or of the huge change with which her life began, but she grew up in small-town Massachusetts during the height of the Cold War, with a big, fine Russian name, Alina Vilenkin.

'So I was constantly telling people I was Russian,' she says, 'and it was a weird time to be Russian. The Soviets were going to send nukes over here to annihilate us, all these scary news stories, and my name just immediately identified me as, well, our country's enemy.'

Alina tells a story of some local kids one Halloween writing 'Commies Go Home' in shaving foam on the family driveway. 'And I felt like I don't want to be this poster child for the Soviet Union,' she says, 'like you're tethering me to a past that I literally don't remember. Lots of people go through life with weird names and it wasn't so much that, but I just felt I was constantly having a conversation with people that I didn't want to have.'

At school, Alina became 'Ally', which resolved things for a while, but that awkward relationship with her own name somehow never quite went away. The years passed and as school and university came and went, her name increasingly became the focus and in some ways the scapegoat for various aspects of her life that Alina longed to change.

'What I really wanted, my dream in life,' she says, 'was to be a singer, but I was overweight and so shy that I just could not get on the stage. I just felt unable to emerge from this chrysalis and the problem was with my name. Because a name is the story of yourself that you tell yourself.' If you don't like that person and don't like that name, then the story you tell yourself about yourself becomes debilitating.'

After university Alina spent three years in Austin, Texas, trying to get started as an indie-rock singer, but with little success and a lot of paralysing nerves. That was when she realised she needed to make a substantial change. Part of that change came with her decision to move to New York City with its vibrant music scene. The other piece of the puzzle – and Alina says this as though it is blindingly obvious, the only real option for someone in her position – 'I needed to change my name.' As she says this, she smiles and makes an expansive gesture with both hands, as though drawing apart a pair of heavy stage curtains.

There now followed many months of what she calls 'internal work'. She mentions the occasion that she received a letter addressed to 'Alina Vileskin' and she roars with laughter, but not, you feel, because it was funny at the time. She magneted the envelope to her refrigerator, 'and it hung there for a year, reminding me, like a nudge to really do it'. Finally upon her arrival in New York in 2000 and her marriage to her long-term boyfriend, she kept Alina but began legal proceedings to swap Vilenkin for her mother's maiden name, Simone.

'I chose it because it's beautiful', she says, glancing out over the Gramercy rooftops. 'I didn't want my husband's name and I'd already had my father's name. I wanted *my* name.' Off she went to court and on 17 November 2000 'the judge banged the gavel,' she says, 'and that was it. I was Alina Simone. It's nice to think I'm only fifteen years old.'

Alina has a winning conversational tic of flipping to and fro between earnest disclosure and whip-quick repartee, one supplying the soul of the story, the other ever so slightly undercutting it. It is almost as if she intuitively knows that the change she undertook began with something akin to a magician's sleight of hand and his show-stopping flourish. Here was an illusory reinvention that nevertheless, for Alina, set the stage for the real change.

Because Alina's life really did seem to pivot on that moment of agency and its curious photo-negative image of the life change that started all this, back when she was a baby. The date of the court order, 17 November 2000, is, Alina says, when she feels her life 'really began'. Her new name was both a gesture of intent and a kind of self-fulfilling prophecy. Remember Ray Bishop and his 'I'm a good man'? Remember Colin Price and his 'shining beacon'? Well, for Alina, what she found in that new self-crafted identity was the courage to pursue what she wanted and the drive to achieve it. She lost weight. She became a singer and, over time, the stage fright left her. She got a record deal and released her first album in 2007. She toured, played big stages, became well known and critically acclaimed. The magic trick had somehow worked.

'Of course, nothing does change when you change your name', she says, unclasping her hair and pinning it back up again. 'You aren't a new person, but I think having that new name was like a commitment to change things, to becoming a new person, like a marriage to your new self. And you do sort of kill your old self, so when people mention Alina Vilenkin now, I do feel she's just not here, like that's the body that was stuffed in the closet. But for me, it was more of a promise to myself' – she sits up straight and adopts a declamatory fairy godmother voice – '"You Shall Become The Singer Alina Simone!" It's like you're setting a stage and the spotlight's on you and it really did enable me to become a person who *was* wholly different. I felt reborn. So that was it. It worked and I didn't do any wacky things after that. I'm still married to the same guy, still have the same face, so I guess', she says, 'we all don't like something about ourselves and maybe we don't like a lot of things about ourselves, but you can't change all of them, or you probably shouldn't. So what are you going to pick? What's it going to be?'

'A self-made man may prefer a self-made name.' So declared a celebrated Manhattan judge to a courtroom just downtown from Alina Simone's apartment. His pronouncement came during the 1923 proceedings in which a young would-be movie mogul called Samuel Goldfish changed his name to Samuel Goldwyn. There is a whiff of snobbery in the judge's pithy take on Goldwyn's career move, but also perhaps a modicum of envy too. For the judge himself was possessed of the somewhat improbable name of Learned Hand. His biographers have alluded to the private discomfort his daft moniker caused him through childhood and into adult life. Besides, Learned Hand was in many ways the very opposite of a self-made man. The scion of a distinguished New York legal family, his life script was half-written for him before he left the cradle.

In social science, something akin to this tension, or that experienced by Alina as she wrestled with her austere Russian name, has been characterised as one between ascribed and achieved status. Ascribed status comes handed down, by dint of gender, ethnicity, the status of one's parents; achieved status is acquired through effort, action, choice. The terms originally come from work in the 1930s by the American anthropologist Ralph Linton and his exploration of open versus closed system societies, those in which one's actions can either elevate or diminish one's status versus those where status is dictated from birth. It does not take a social scientist to tell you that even in a culture that encourages and expects self-determination, each of us nevertheless meets the world and makes a life within it according to a blend of achieved and ascribed attributes. This is true both in the academic sense first outlined by Linton and in a more fluid sense as well. It is a duality that recalls the quarrel in psychology over the elasticity or fixity of our personalities and also the flip between organic change and that driven by agency.

The contemporary sociologist Anthony Giddens, famous for his study of the conditions of modernity, has taken the idea an intriguing step further. He argues that in today's post-traditional societies, where achieved identity is the norm, every one of us has become the author of our own biography, the narrator of what Giddens calls 'an ongoing story about the self'. Identity is now a self-made commodity. *'What to do? How to act? Who to be?'* These are questions, says Giddens, that every one of us must answer. Even those not given to navel-gazing will make manifold identity-shaping decisions throughout their lives about how they spend their time at work and at play, what they wear, who they love, what they believe in. This, argues Giddens, is both our blessing and our curse, both a path to self-fulfilment and a fresh source of angst as to whether we are getting it right. Above all, this new world of self-made identity has, at its very core, change as a lifestyle choice.

Perhaps that is why recent statistics from the UK Deed Poll Service demonstrate a steep rise – between 10 and 12 per cent year-on-year since 2001 – in the numbers of people choosing to give the protagonist of their own life stories a new name. What was for the Harry Houdinis and Sam Goldwyns of this world a daring leap is now part of the repertoire of magic tricks that an individual hungry for change can dip into – proof that a certain form of metamorphosis can and does take place.

Simone Mello-Perez was, she says, 'shopping for a new name' in late 2011, when she went to a gallery opening at which Alina Simone and her band were playing. A Brazilian lawyer long resident in Manhattan, Simone had had one hell of a year. Following a course of IVF and a failed pregnancy – not, sadly, her first – she had stumbled one Saturday morning on her husband in the kitchen of their apartment talking to a woman on Skype. He had snapped the laptop shut and gone out for a walk, but by the end of the afternoon he had answered Simone's questions about the woman by asking for a divorce. That was in January. By March the papers were signed and the ten-year marriage was over.

Simone was 'heartbroken', but she also realised that this

was an opportunity for 'a completely new life'. Her husband had been controlling, she says, and she unhealthily dependent, risk-averse, very fearful of change. But now this personal cataclysm had been visited upon her, so here was a chance to begin a metamorphosis of her own making.

'And in fact I got a tattoo,' she adds, touching one angular shoulder, 'a butterfly on my back, because, well, those wings would never, ever, ever be taken away by anybody.'

The butterfly tattoo was swiftly followed by a decision that a new name was needed. Like the first Alina, she says this as if it were the most obvious choice in the world.

'Clearly I wanted to get rid of his name,' she says, fiddling with a strand of blonde hair, 'but I thought that Simone Mello didn't represent me either. That was the person I was before the marriage, my childhood in Brazil. So I wasn't either of these other two people any more. I needed an identity for this new person that was just being born and I had the chance to choose how I wanted to make that person.'

Spotting the cover of one of Alina Simone's records at the gallery opening – and before she had either seen Alina or heard so much as a bar of the music itself – sparked an epiphany. 'When I saw it, I had no doubt that was *my* name,' she says, as if oblivious to how extraordinary this sounds. The very next day she began asking people to call her Alina. At a courthouse in Manhattan, some months later, the second Alina Simone was born. 'And I felt light, like I had no past, like I could build and be whoever I wanted to be. I was born that day, really.'

The new Alina is, she maintains, more 'courageous' than Simone ever was, her new name 'the fuel that powers that decision to be a different person, because we are many different people in one person.' But being a new person is not always a magic trick. It is hard work and something Alina is still trying, in her words, 'to live up to'. For you can change

74

some things profoundly, but not everything, so you must choose with care. In 2014 Alina moved back home to Brazil to start again. New York was too full of ghosts and it is from a small, sun-drenched flat in São Paulo that she is speaking today. 'So I'm still building it,' she says, 'that new life, still looking for happiness. As everyone is, I guess' and she turns her head to look out of the window onto the noisy street below.

Alina Simone, 'the Original' as the second Alina calls her, says she found it 'a bit weird' when she heard through a mutual acquaintance of Simone Mello-Perez's adoption of her name. Yet her curiosity was piqued and the two met for a drink in New York. 'I almost felt I knew her', says the second Alina, 'and it was nice to learn that it wasn't really her name either.' Meanwhile, the first Alina was won over by the second's 'indomitable optimism' and says she is now delighted to share her name with this woman with the butterfly tattoo. 'She really needed that name, you know?'

And you can picture the two Alina Simones through the frosty window of the bar that cold December evening: one dark, one blonde, one Russian, one Brazilian, two very different lives, two very different reasons to change, but a single conduit, an odd little magic trick, for doing so.

7

THE EYE

Can you recollect the marvel of your first journey in an aeroplane? The sense of reckless acceleration on the runway, the deep tug in your lower back as the front wheels lift, resolved almost immediately into a heavy smoothness, your ears stuffed with the antiseptic hum of the aircraft, as the world below disconnects. Cars like the one in which you arrived at the airport, filled with squabbling families and harried businessmen, soon look like toys, the cavernous terminal building with all its crowds and shops and officials in uniform now a paltry shoebox and the city beyond little more than a smudge of grey and green.

The revelation is perhaps at its most intense in cloud-wreathed northern climes. For you ascend into an embrace of misty, grey closeness, where it feels as if no one can see or care about you, and then all at once, you are above the clouds and you realise that the sun is shining up there. The sky is blue, in spite of the drizzle you left down on the ground. It is a whole new way of looking at the world, very different from, but no less true than, the one you left behind when you got on the plane. If only you could bottle that feeling, for change is often underpinned by exactly that kind of revelation.

Christopher Liu changes how people see the world. And indeed, sometimes, he changes not just *how* they see it, but the very fact that they can. Liu is a consultant ophthalmologist at Sussex Eye Hospital in Brighton and one of the UK's most distinguished eye surgeons. A working life contained within the globe of this small, complex organ and with such tiny margins for error encourages introspection, he says. It forces you to face your own limitations and carries a great burden of responsibility, but it is nevertheless for Liu an abiding passion. It is work that changes lives. 'Oh yes, it definitely does that', he says, quietly.

Liu's specialism is the front of the eye, the cornea, a structure just half a millimetre thick yet essential to our window on the world. Much of his routine surgery is for cataracts, but five or six times a year the softly spoken physician undertakes a bizarre, complex and highly invasive procedure known as osteo-odonto-keratoprosthesis (OOKP). He is the only surgeon in the UK to perform it. OOKP is a surgical treatment for certain complicated forms of corneal blindness. It relies on bypassing the dysfunctional or damaged cornea of one eye with a tiny Perspex optical cylinder which the body is tricked into accepting via an outlandish deceit, one that sounds more like a detail from a Dalí painting than cutting-edge modern medicine.

During the first of two operations scar tissue is removed from the damaged cornea. Then the eye is covered with a flap of skin taken from inside the patient's cheek. Next, a canine tooth is harvested from the jaw, along with its root and a small block of surrounding bone. This is fashioned into a kind of window frame and the optical cylinder inserted into it. The tiny chimera is then planted under the lower lid muscle of the other eye, where it must remain for some months while the body spins tissue around it. Everyone waits. Finally, during the second operation, a hole is cut in the cheek tissue and the damaged cornea beneath it. The tooth with its tiny artificial window is fetched out from beneath the other eye, now clothed in enough flesh to bamboozle its new host, and is fixed into the hole. For between two-thirds and three-quarters of patients the visual world now leaks back in their hitherto sightless lives, as if in proof of the extent to which our sensory experience of the world can be transformed.

The recovery of sight is an ancient symbol of profound redemptive change. Think of the line from the Bible, 'I was blind but now I see', made iconic almost to the point of cliché by 'Amazing Grace'. But for Liu – although, intriguingly, he does mention that he is a religious man who feels he has been given 'a gift and an opportunity to help my fellow humans' – salvation of this sort is not something simply dished out from on high. It is not an instance of acquiescent change, of submitting first to malady and then to cure. Instead, Christopher Liu characterises the decision to go through the ordeal and the uncertainty of OOKP surgery as driven by very careful and deliberate agency on the part of the blind patient. Rather than a quick-fix remedy, it is a calculated act of choosing the chance to see, one for which the patient must be psychologically equipped. As Mark Twain wrote in one of his short stories, 'You can't depend on your eyes when your imagination is out of focus.'

'You make vision. It's weird, but it's imagination, I think, and you make pictures, shapes, stories out of things. Fill in a lot of gaps. People's faces, you imagine them. Have you ever done that? When you're on the phone to somebody, you picture them, don't you? You never have a moment when you don't picture them, do you? So that's exactly how a blind person operates, or how I did anyway. Every day you have in your mind what seeing is like, every day, everything you do.'

Shander Herian is one of Christopher Liu's patients. Now in his early fifties, Shander was nine when he contracted Stevens-Johnson Syndrome, a rare but life-threatening skin condition. 'It's like somebody took you', he says, easing back into a soft curving sofa, 'and dropped you in a vat of hot water.' The skin bubbles up and falls off, taking fingernails, toenails and tear ducts with it. Shander spent four months in Wolverhampton General Hospital, dangerously ill at first, and then bandaged from head to toe. Another three months followed in a specialist eye hospital, for, as his other symptoms stabilised, the inability to make tears was causing grave concern for his sight. Without lubrication, the surface of the eye is gradually scarred by the action of blinking, and over time the cornea thickens, growing blood vessels until, says Shander, 'it's like the skin on your hand'.

That is what happened to him. At first he could see perfectly well – he describes in great detail a tenth birthday card the nurses gave him in hospital – but over the four years that followed, the visual world gradually retreated. First it was the blackboard at school and Shander moved to the front of the class; next it was the football on the street with his friends, so he rode his bike instead; when that became impossible, or rather, dangerous, he retreated indoors; finally, it was his much-loved comics, *The Dandy*, *The Beano*, *The Beezer*, all now lost to him.

These years were punctuated with dozens of operations, medications and other interventions, as his parents left no stone unturned to save their son's sight. But in the end Shander moved to a residential school for the blind, learned Braille and finally in his late teens he started, he says, 'to think well this is it now, that's how it's going to be for the rest of my life'.

At this point, in response to a well-worn question about being 'plunged into darkness' – a misconception-cum-cliché about blindness that visually impaired people face all the time – Shander replies mildly, 'No, there's never been darkness. If you ask any blind person, there's almost always the sensation of light, sunshine coming in through a window' – he stirs his spoon in his coffee – 'maybe it's the heat on your face, I don't know. So it was as if you fill this room with steam, like a thick, heavy, grey fog', and he looks about the large, bright living-room with its cinema TV, its glass coffee table held up by a cast iron nymph with head bowed.

Like Hyppolite Ntigurirwa, Shander found a way through his difficulties in part because he began to excel at school and later at college. His memory became outstanding, super-powered. His confidence and independence grew. He 'found out about girls' – a big belly laugh – went drinking, had fun and, as everyone was blind or partially sighted around him, that acute sense of being different lessened. At home, his parents' pride in his achievements, along with a growing acceptance on their part of his blindness, began to shift the emphasis. Visitors now talked *to* him and less *about* him. 'I suppose that's what you call having your own identity', he says. 'Whatever situation you're in, you make the best of it. I really believe that this cracking machine, the human body, just adapts and your psychology does as well. So I was happy, I was flourishing.'

Shander qualified in computer programming in 1986 when he was twenty-four and from there he began to make a life for himself. Less than a decade later, after much early hardship and a good deal of work, he and his now wife, Gurjeet, had built from nothing one of the biggest IT suppliers in the Midlands. They bought the old Avery Scales factory in Wolverhampton town centre and renamed it Herian House, quite a leap for the blind son of an immigrant metalworker. 'I was really quite proud of what I'd achieved, to be honest', he says. He shows a photograph of the gleaming Mercedes S-class that he and his wife used to park on the meter outside their shop – 'I thought I'd arrived really' – and he grins.

One morning early in 1996, a local optician to whom Shander supplied PCs came rushing into Herian House waving a trade magazine in which there was an article about Christopher Liu and the OOKP procedure.

'There's this Chinese guy in Brighton,' the optician had enthused, 'you've got to go and see him.'

Shander was unmoved. 'I'd had so many knock-backs, like thirty, maybe more, so I said, "Oh, ignore it, I ain't going to bother with that."' But the optician was like a dog with a bone and eventually Shander came round. There followed more than twelve months of consultations, quarrels with the local authority over funding and lengthy debates over which eye to perform the procedure on, right up until the night before the first operation.

And this is where you get a sense of how strongly Shander was in the driving seat of this choice, how very deliberate and carefully considered it was. For contrary to the doctors' initial suggestion, he was adamant that they should perform the procedure not on his 'good eye', the one through which he could detect light and dark – 'I wasn't going to sacrifice that', he says – but on the eye that was entirely sightless. 'This one', he says and tapping the edge of his large dark glasses on the left, he smiles.

In March 1997, Shander underwent the first stage of the OOKP procedure. The aftermath was all pain and no sight. He hooks up his lip with a finger and shows the gaping hole in his mouth. Then came the long three-month wait.

'And at no time did I ever really believe that it would work', he adds.

'Didn't you?'

'No', says Shander, swiping the air with his hand. 'There were certainly no thoughts that this is going to be one of them miracles. It was just another of these routines I'd been through a hundred times before and people kept saying, "But what if it does?" So I just thought maybe I'll be able to walk around a bit better, pick up a cup or something. I didn't think there was a massive change coming, certainly not that.' Shander turns his head away and one lens of his dark glasses catches the reflection of a pigeon flying past outside the window.

Shander Herian's story is about a very particular kind of change, built neither on soaring hope nor on plunging despair, neither shining beacon nor burning platform (to recall Colin Price's characterisation). Like the other stories we have met so far, it entwines the external forces of change that turn our lives upside down and the inner grit by which we wrestle back some agency from the cosmos to change our own lives. Yet in Shander's case, this choice was simply to open one door to change, with little sense of what might be found on the other side, but an intuition that it would be somehow bloody-minded to maintain the status quo. And in that, there may be some change wisdom for us all.

The Greek biographer and historian Plutarch gives an account of an ancient thought experiment that divided philosophers of old. It relates to the ship of the mythical founder-king of Athens, Theseus, and to whether many years of preservation and restoration had compromised its claim to be the Ship of Theseus at all. If one by one, as the years passed, each decaying timber of the trusty vessel had been replaced, was it still the same boat? It is a question that has vexed philosophers ever since, with no clear consensus reached, and it finds voice in contemporary philosophical debates about personal identity. You will catch an echo here of Epicharmus' gag about the pebbles, but more serious-minded folk have put it like this: if our identity resides chiefly within the physical continuity of our bodies, and given that each cell of the body is replaced many times in the course of a life, to what extent is it true to say that the child and the man he is many years later are one and the same person? Answers on a postcard, please.

This question of difference and sameness hangs about in the background of all personal change and we shall return to it anon, but for the time being, let us savour a rather poetic taste of the numerous latter-day iterations of Theseus and his shonky ship. It comes from the work of a German philosopher called Otto Neurath and relates to his non-foundational theory of scientific knowledge. Now stay with me here, because it also offers a striking image of what anyone undertaking change in their own life has, in reality, to contend with.

'There is no tabula rasa', wrote Neurath. 'We are like sailors who must rebuild their ship on the open sea, never able to dismantle it in dry-dock and to reconstruct it there from its best components.'

Think of Ray Bishop and his return to prison, or of Ed Coxon's point that 'life is in session', and you realise that in Neurath's insight lies the central real-time challenge of choosing to change. The extent to which it will work is by no means a given.

Like a sailor, then, on the open sea, Shander Herian waited the twelve weeks and duly went into hospital for the second OOKP operation. He had been told not to expect too much in the early days and that his sight, if it returned at all, would do so gradually.

The day after the operation, Christopher Liu came to see Shander for the removal of the bandages. The nurses took the dressings away and Shander says he could see nothing more than 'a bright grey'. Liu stepped in to clean up the eye.

'And as he's cleaning it with this little cotton bud,' says Shander, 'I could suddenly see his tie, gold with a black pattern on it and then I could see his face and that was it. Literally in the time it's taken me to just say that. And you look around and you can see everything. You can see for miles.' He pauses and says it again. '*You can see.* It was a sunny day. There was a tiny window, but it just seemed like somebody had flooded the room with light. It was sharp and I sat up in the bed looking around because the doctors are talking to you and you're saying, "Yeah I can see" and they're like, "How much can you see? Can you see these fingers? Can you see that there?"' – he whispers – '"Yeah I can." It was incredible and it just goes to show, doesn't it? You don't know what's around the corner.'

Little expecting this jubilant outcome, the Herian family had stayed in Wolverhampton, but now Shander's two daughters, then aged five and eight, were fetched from school by their mother and they all drove the four hours down to Brighton to visit the father and husband who had never seen them before in his life.

'Yeah, that was a goose pimply bit, that was,' says Shander, his voice a little hoarse for a moment, 'seeing them for the first time'. He clears his throat and thinks for a moment. 'It's funny, because that's exactly how I'd always imagined them to look. I know the lad who drove them down, Mark who worked for me, he looked completely different to what I'd expected, but Gurjeet and the little girls – '. He leaves the sentence unfinished with a little shake of his head, although later he says that they remain his 'favourite sight'.

Over the weeks that followed, every day was an intense, vivid experience of colour and beauty, so different from his recollection of the beige 1970s and tempered only by the nagging question of how long it would last. That was now eighteen years ago and Shander says, 'Being able to see is, I think, a miracle. And one thing I do know is that I would hate to go back. If I could ever not see now, I don't think I'd be able to cope.'

Which is not to say that Shander's sight is perfect. His one working eye has a limited visual field and can only see in two, not three, dimensions. The eye itself looks, in his words, 'gruesome' and he still hides behind the dark glasses he has worn all his life. His super-powered memory left him overnight, as if the imagination that had sustained his years of blindness and fuelled this bold leap back into the world of sight was simply 'overwhelmed'. Every change, even those we choose, brings a shred or two of loss, as we have seen. Even today, Shander has trouble remembering faces, occasionally even his beloved wife's. He also has plenty of what he calls 'blind habits' – 'I touch everything' – and he still, strangely, dreams as a sightless man. Yet Shander's overwhelming sense is one of profound and transformative good fortune, a luck that so many of his blind friends cannot share and one that has taught him humility, adaptability and gratitude for having had what he calls 'more lives than most'. His is a story of change in which a limber and open imagination – willing to take a risk, make a choice, unbolt the door to a different life – played as central a role as the fine-fingered skill of the surgeon.

'I do feel that I'm a better person for having been blind for twenty-five years', he says, touching his big black glasses again instinctively. 'I don't begrudge it because I've seen a side of life that everybody else can't. In order to appreciate wealth, you've got to be poor, haven't you? And so what I'll find incredibly awesome is something that you'll just pass without a second thought. A sunset, the sky at night, or yesterday I sat here watching some pigeons on the fence, just some fat pigeons, but taking a pause and actually seeing what's happening. There are loads of little daily things I notice that everybody else would just walk by. You're trying to soak it up. And it makes me glad that I can.'

8

THE HEART

Shall we break for a song? If you have a viol handy, that will do. Or a lute. And maybe a recorder would be nice. For this song comes from Shakespeare's *Merchant of Venice*, where it offers some incidental music at a moment of high romantic jeopardy. Bassanio, a noble but impecunious young suitor for the fragrant hand of wealthy Portia, must choose according to the decree of her late father between three metal caskets. This is a bit like a Renaissance Venice version of a fruit machine: he who makes the right choice wins the girl and her fortune. Already the princes of Morocco and Aragon have gambled and lost. Now as Bassanio deliberates, considering gold versus silver versus lead, and as Portia who loves him holds her breath, a couple of minstrels among her entourage attempt to lighten the mood with a tart little ditty about love:

> Tell me where is fancy bred,
> Or in the heart or in the head,
> How begot, how nourishèd?

Reply, reply.
It is engend'red in the eyes,
With gazing fed; and fancy dies
In the cradle where it lies.

There follows a splendidly silly refrain of *ding-dong-dells* and you will be delighted to learn that at length Bassanio makes the correct choice; the clue to 'lead' was in the rhyme and he wins his beloved.

Of course, the song's pat conclusion that love is both spawned and soured by what we see is cynical at best – Shander Herian's love for Gurjeet was neither conceived nor sustained in the eye, was it? And yet the questions posed here remain fundamental ones about what is arguably life's greatest change agent: love.

For it is in love that external forces of change and individual agency collide in a shower of fireworks. Why do we fall in love? How can love be sustained over time? And where does it come from, heart or mind? Well, according to contemporary neuroscience, we finally have the 'reply, reply': the heart is simply in the head. Indeed, answers to time-honoured inquiry about the provenance and course of our affections have come thick and fast in recent years. Brain scans have mapped in sultry colour the ebb and flow of our romantic lives from sexual attraction to heartbreak.

It was 1975 when Roxy Music sang that love is a drug, and some forty years later the biological anthropologist and Kinsey research fellow, Helen Fisher, was moved to agree. Love as it appears in an MRI scan, according to her research, bears all the neurological hallmarks of addiction. The first-love production of serotonin, norepinephrine and dopamine in the reward circuits of the brain mirrors the effects of cocaine, while heartbreak apparently elicits a response within the brain that is akin to drug withdrawal.

A trio of psychiatrists in San Francisco make a related but more nuanced argument, one that combines brain chemistry with perhaps a little more of Shakespeare's poetry. In their *A General Theory of Love*, Thomas Lewis, Fari Amini and Richard Lannon posit a phenomenon they call 'limbic resonance'. The word 'limbic' relates to a complex system of cortical and subcortical structures that sit deep within the brain. It is this limbic system that filters our lives for emotional content, weaving memories, feeding dreams and generating feelings from it. If love is on the cards, then the limbic brain certainly has a hand to play.

'Limbic resonance', as the psychiatrists have coined it, is what then happens when emotions are shared between two limbic brains, when eyes meet, hands touch, hearts chime together. It is, they write, 'a symphony of mutual exchange and internal adaptation whereby two mammals become attuned to each other's inner state'. And here is the central conceit: love and the associated limbic resonance with another human being then actively *changes the structure of our brain*, with all the musical reciprocity of a close-sung harmony.

Neuronal pathways are established and then reinforced, learned by repetition, according to a model of synaptic plasticity first identified in 1949 by the Canadian neuropsychologist Donald Hebb. Hebbian Learning, as it became known, is the model of adaptation that allows our brains to alter with experience, 'transforming us from who we *were* into who we *are*'. It is, according to Lewis, Amini and Lannon, the mechanism by which we learn to love in the first place, cradled in our mothers' arms. While those early experiences suggest the key in which future melodies may be sung, that pattern of feelings we call love remains ever receptive to 'limbic revision', new configurations, new harmonies that occur when our limbic brain makes beautiful music with another. In other words, if you want to identify the extent and the locus of a change of heart, then limbic revision is as good a place as any to begin.

It is an idea that offers both a model of profound change and also one of constancy, a lovely counterpoint to the reward-driven coke-fiend characterisation of our romantic drives; for limbic resonance not only establishes the neuronal pathways of togetherness but can also over time strengthen them. As Lewis, Amini and Lannon conclude, 'Who we are and who we become depends, in part, on whom we love.' It is a line that could almost be set to music.

Joanne Fleisher used to think that she was incapable of falling in love. Which is not to say that she had not given it her very best shot.

Joanne's teenage years in suburban Philadelphia were full of dating, lots of crushes, lots of making out. 'I did', she says with the barest suggestion of a twinkle, 'everything that was expected of me and not with any difficulty.' When she left home and went away to college in Boston, in the mid-1960s, Joanne went, she says, 'a little bit crazy wild. I broke loose from my home life and I dated *a lot* of men. I was very sexual, a little out of control, but I had a great time, because I never, ever fell in love with any of the guys I was dating. I just' – she chooses her word – 'enjoyed them. I had no desire to marry them and so they were happy too.'

The behaviour that seventy-year-old Joanne is describing so drily has perhaps more in common with the addictive model of the romantic impulse than with deep limbic resonance, but after college she describes how she began to feel 'a strong need' to simmer down. So she called up an ex-boyfriend from high school called Bob.

'I knew I wanted to get married', she says, as if that were the natural corollary to such a telephone call. 'I wanted to settle down and I knew Bob was a good guy, very responsible, very smart. I was not in love with him, but I cared about him and I felt like it would be a good marriage. So I called him at law school and it just went very quickly from there. He asked me to marry him fairly soon after that and at twenty-two I got married.'

Sometimes when we look back at old relationships that did not work, we realise that we were not in love, although at the time we thought we were – or is it that we were in love, but can no longer imagine how or why? At any rate, if you put this slippage of romantic memory to Joanne, she comes back instantly and with great certainty.

'No, I thought there was something wrong with me,' she says, 'not consciously perhaps, but I'd never had the falling in love experience that other people were talking about. I felt like I wasn't capable of it. I guess there was an edge of detachment, just something' – she shrugs – 'a little missing, you know? And I wasn't ever going to have that kind of experience. I felt excited about getting married and I'd say I loved him, but I didn't feel *in love*.'

The marriage went well at first and after a few years Bob and Joanne had two daughters, eighteen months apart. But as the 1970s got under way, Joanne came across counterculture for the first time – hippies, feminism, the sexual revolution, all of it a world away from the 'very conventional environment' in which she had grown up and lived thus far. 'My curiosity was really piqued,' she says, 'and it was the beginning of a shift for me.' At home, cracks began to appear in the life that she and Bob had made. 'Restless', as she says, Joanne asked for an open marriage, the kind of arrangement in which many of her friends were enthusiastically engaged at the time. Bob acquiesced, 'but he gave me some no-nos and one of the no-nos was not-with-a-woman. I don't know where that was coming from, because I wasn't moving in that direction.'

But move in that direction Joanne would. She describes how, over these years, she was encountering lesbians for the first time in her life, having had little idea when she was growing up that there was any such thing. 'I just had an intense curiosity about them,' she says, twisting a bead in her necklace, 'and I would ask them to tell me about their lives.' Joanne belonged to a women's group, among them a lesbian with whom Joanne struck up a friendship. Eventually they became lovers.

'I guess I was doing this somewhat lightly,' she says, 'not thinking it was going to have that huge an impact, but as soon as I got involved with her in that way, I just fell in love and it was very quick. It's trite to say, but I felt like I was coming home and it felt comfortable. It felt right, very intimate, very loving, very sensual. It was all that *In Love* stuff. I was just swept off my feet' – she smiles – 'but I'd had no inkling whatsoever before other than that curiosity and I still didn't believe that I was a lesbian.'

'Didn't you? Why not?'

'I thought lesbians seemed' – she thinks for a second – 'well, Other. I lived in the suburbs. I had a station wagon and a husband and two kids and I looked very, very middle America. So it was an accident that happened. I mean it was also a discovery that happened, but not something I expected. And I kept it secret for a while, but not for long because I'd never lied. I didn't want to live two lives. I wanted to choose one.'

Time for another song of love. The orchestra is lilting a soft, schmaltzy two-step and across a dance floor crowded with slick gents in evening dress and monochrome dames in gowns, sidles Fred Astaire. On his arm is an anonymous brunette, but in his eye is the swaying luminescence of Ginger Rogers, across the floor. As Fred sashays his way alongside Ginger and her partner, a man who looks like he should be advertising hair pomade, Fred, with bright, daring smile and raised brow, pipes up:

> Must you dance ev'ry dance
> With the same fortunate man?
> You have danced with him
> Since the music began.
> Won't you change partners
> And dance with me?

And of course, in the film's happily-ever-after, Ginger does just that, swapping one fiancé, the scowling man with the hair, for fleet-footed, silver-tongued Fred Astaire.

In real life, Ginger Rogers changed partners a number of times with five marriages and five divorces in forty years. Because sometimes in love we get it wrong, and sometimes we simply change our minds. Love is not always Shakespeare's 'ever-fixèd mark/That looks on tempests and is never shaken'. Quite often, in fact, it looks on minor squalls and is shuddered to pieces. As we have seen, these tender metamorphoses are evidenced within the very fabric of our emotional being, the neural pathways of our supple brains. They are proof, in their way, of the extent to which we can be transformed while remaining firmly ourselves and of how we do so at the point of convergence between outside change and that within.

Yet a change of sexual orientation is often instinctively regarded as perhaps a more profound change of amatory direction than any other. This is especially so in a case like

Joanne Fleisher's, where, as she says, it was not simply a matter of surrendering to a desire she had suppressed all her life so much as opening the door to another way of living and of loving. While quarrels rage over the genetic origins, or otherwise, of homosexuality, mopping up along the way much fevered and often ugly political debate, others have argued that sexuality is simply more fluid, more malleable than we habitually think. This is not an overture to the unpalatable lunacy of so-called 'gay conversion therapy'; that will get no airtime here. But what is fascinating is the way in which this fluidity, this ability to change, stands in opposition to the idea of simply being in or outside of the closet or even at a defined point on the Kinsey scale that runs from 0 to 6, exclusively heterosexual to exclusively homosexual. Particularly intriguing are the numerous studies that have shown that such fluidity is more common among women than among men, although not exclusively so. In 2000, the social psychologist Roy Baumeister gave a name to what he called 'erotic plasticity': the extent to which one's sexual drive is affected by socio-cultural and situational factors. Baumeister went on to hypothesise that women have naturally higher levels of erotic plasticity than men. It was the developmental psychologist and prominent feminist Lisa Diamond who then brought the idea of female sexual fluidity into the mainstream. She argues that changes in sexual orientation identity are not voluntary, in the sense of a lifestyle choice – *Which handbag shall I buy?* – but that the focus and shape of desire can nevertheless flex and shift in a way that is more complex, more multilayered, one might even say more musical, than our conventional rubric of phases, denials and ratings would allow.

The point is this: that any of us – man or woman, gay or straight, looking for love or leaving it behind or indeed just rolling along, trying to keep that ol' flame alight – could do worse than to be mindful of this mercurial quality of erotic love. For it can reinvent the heart's desire, filling it with new songs.

There is a long silence as Joanne Fleisher considers a question about whether the Joanne who had now fallen in love with a woman was the more 'true' of her 'two lives'.

'I mean, some people would say I was a lesbian from birth,' she says, 'but I don't think we're one thing. I really don't. We are many things. We have many identities and we grow, we learn through the shifting tides of what happens in life. I think we're too constricted by these ideas of what sexuality is and how it's defined and how it's limited to this or to that. And I guess the good thing about following your heart – in any manner – is that it's a way of feeling free to express yourself as authentically as you can.'

Joanne Fleisher's first love lasted just a few months, but in that time she told her husband. So there it was and she did not know what to do next. She had never thought of leaving Bob. The children were still small, just seven and nine. She felt, she says, as if she were lining up to destroy all their lives. Joanne went into therapy and spent some months vacillating 'back and forth, back and forth'. But something had come apart. Without even the limbic memory of past passion to shore up the present, her motivation to make the marriage work faded away, like the last note of a song that is over. 'It was too late', says Joanne and then she says it again. 'It was too late. I had lost it. I had no idea what my sexuality was, but I decided that I absolutely had to explore it.'

This move to lever the door ajar is where agency and choice then came into play. How to do it? How to do this thing? The hesitation was not, as we have already learned elsewhere, a resistance to change so much as a fear of loss. The practical, financial and emotional implications were all, says Joanne, 'terrifying, but part of who I am is a person who goes for the thing I think I need to do and I did just believe that I would find a way'. And find a way she did. Quite simply, Joanne talked to as many people who had faced this dilemma as she could, absorbing their stories as a kind of 'research' for rewriting her own. It was a process that has much in common with the experiment in this very book.

'I guess I wanted to hear success stories,' she says, 'because you know you're moving towards something different, but you don't know what different really looks like or feels like. You know very well what you're leaving and that's hard because you know you're losing something, but what you're going towards is the unknown and finally getting the courage to take the leap requires a certain amount of hope and a certain amount of imagination. So maybe talking to people gives you that hope, that imagination. It gives you a sense that it can be done.'

In 1979 Bob and Joanne parted. It was, she says, the hardest decision she has ever had to make and the biggest change she has ever, in her seventy years, deliberately made. 'And divorce is tough, particularly on children,' says Joanne, 'I'm not going to sugar-coat that.' But somehow the family got through it. Only three months later Joanne met and fell in love with Judy, the woman with whom she would raise her children and spend the next thirty-one years of her life. That romantic serendipity may, in part, account for why Joanne says, 'Yes, I agonised, but once I'd made that decision, I never looked back. And my experience of the change, because it was such a monumental change, began to change me, you know? Because I was happier and I felt freer.'

After half a lifetime together Joanne Fleisher's partner died of cancer in 2011. 'So my life has changed again,' she says, looking at her hands for a moment. 'I wish Judy were alive, I wish I was still in love with her, but that's not the way it's working, so I guess there's something about understanding that when you're faced with these things, it's part of life. We have this illusion that things are stable, but in reality everything in life changes, everything. So the thing is to be able to see change not as a tragedy, but rather to look for how you can adjust and learn and grow from it. I guess you have to find a way of becoming comfortable with the uncertainty, not staring too far into the future and paying a lot of attention to the present.' She looks up and she smiles brightly. 'Yeah, I think that's the answer. And even though my old friends say it's crazy, I'm dating again.'

9

THE HEAD

David Hume did not much go in for dating. Serious and roly-poly – indeed, seriously roly-poly – the great philosopher of the Scottish Enlightenment was a lifelong bachelor in spite of his famous contention that reason is 'a slave of the passions'. In February 1761 Hume replied to a letter of breathless admiration for his work from a literary hostess in Paris. 'I have rusted', he wrote back, 'amid books and study, have been little engaged in the active and not much in the pleasurable scenes of life' and off the letter went from grey Edinburgh to the gilded salon of the Comtesse de Boufflers. Yet Hume may have been overstating it somewhat, for he accepted her invitation upon his arrival in Paris in 1763 and the two embarked on an intimate friendship. Soon Hume harboured a few of those aforementioned passions for the blousy charms of the Comtesse. Whether they were ever consummated, history does not relate – she led him what in Scotland they call 'a merry dance' – but it is fun to imagine a bit of limbic revision going on beneath the curls of Hume's powdered wig.

At any rate, David Hume may not be the man to consult on matters of the heart, but on the workings of the head he is one of the kings of Enlightenment thought. Having devoted much of his life to the empirical study of our minds, one of his most influential and boldest ideas was his 'bundle theory' of human identity.

Laid out in his *Treatise of Human Nature,* written in 1739, when he was just twenty-eight, bundle theory is a kick in the teeth to any unified notion of the Self. In fact, according to Hume, there is no such thing. 'For my part,' he wrote, 'when I enter most intimately into what I call myself, I always stumble on some particular perception or other, of heat, cold, light or shade, love or hatred, pain or pleasure. I can never catch myself at any time without a perception, and can never observe anything but the perception.' Please, go ahead and try it yourself; you will find that the portly Scot has a point. Going to sleep or dropping dead seem the only ways to escape the stream of perceptions. This observation then led Hume to make a startling leap, more reminiscent of Buddhist philosophy or modern existentialism than of ordered eighteenth-century thinking: that we 'are nothing but a bundle ... of different perceptions which succeed each other with an inconceivable rapidity, and are in perpetual flux and movement'.

Thus Hume put change at the centre of human nature, arguing that the mind is nothing more than 'a kind of theatre' in which these kaleidoscopic responses to the world are played out. Remember William James on the mind as theatre in Chapter 1? Well, it may be from Hume that he harvested this idea, but what Hume did with it that was so bold was to drive it to the most radical conclusion: 'The identity which we ascribe to the mind of man', he wrote, 'is only a fictitious one.' It is a figment of our imaginations.

Had he donned his heavy frock coat and travelled two and half centuries into the future and many miles to the south, to a modest house on a leafy suburban street in Leeds in 2015, one wonders what David Hume would have made of the Holmes family. For sure, their experience of recent years stands as evidence to how profoundly the perceptions of the mind can change the person in whose head that mind is lodged. On the face of it, their story confounds any fantasy we might harbour that there is an immutable essence to who we are. Yet it is hard not to feel that Hume's apparent ease with dismantling personal identity altogether might be challenged by the Holmes family. For their capacity for sustained and yet adaptive love from the midst of a firestorm of change, their real-world need to believe that identity of some sort exists and that it matters, turns out to be as persuasive as any treatise.

It is Peter Holmes who answers the door with an uncertain but sunny smile, his elder sister Vikki at his shoulder. Their mother, Sofia, is at work, but their father, Robert, a retired newspaper editor, has already run through the skeleton of the story on the drive from the railway station. In 2011, when the family was on holiday visiting Sofia's Serbian family, Peter and Vikki were taken jet-skiing by their cousins on the River Sava in Belgrade. Peter's jet-ski crashed and he sustained a blunt blow to the front of his head that nearly killed him. He spent ten days in a coma and over the months of treatment and rehabilitation that followed, the family and Peter himself had to come to terms with the fact that the injury to his brain had profoundly changed Peter's personality.

'The specialist said that we were just waiting for Peter's brain to reboot,' said Robert as he parked the car outside their home, 'but four years is a long time rebooting. I remember a friend of mine at work saying you just have to wait to get Peter back, but I know we're not going to get the old Peter back. Anyway, here we are. This is our house.'

When Peter answers the door, there are no obvious signs that he has suffered such a devastating head injury. He is a tall, good-looking lad, in T-shirt and jeans, his face unscarred, his movements easy and his small talk about the journey, the weather, how you take your tea, much as it would be with any other young man of twenty-one: not exactly slick, but puppyish and friendly.

Peter and Vikki, both home from university for the holidays, settle in the living-room and Robert brings in cups of tea. There are large family photographs on the walls, those informal studio portraits shot at jaunty angles against a white background. They were taken not long before the accident and in the pictures everyone is smiling or laughing. Today there are also lots of smiles and laughter, much finishing of one another's sentences, family in-jokes and asides to each other's stories. Yet the sense that the family are still reeling from the magnitude of what happened to them in August 2011 is palpable.

They skirt around it for a while by talking about what Peter was like before the accident. He was fun, laid-back, sporty. 'Like, Arsenal-mad', says his father. 'And messy. You were very messy', says Vikki, turning to explain, 'He's very tidy now.' 'Everything in his room', says Robert, 'like this' and he mimes things laid out in rows. Above all, they say, Peter was incredibly close to his twin brother, Alex, now studying in Portugal. 'We knew each other off by heart,' Peter says, 'very, very, very close.' There is a pause. 'Yes, it's difficult, isn't it?' says Robert, 'talking about what you were like back then.'

They talk about the summer of the accident in Serbia, the huge family lunch only the day before with their great-uncle in the orchard outside Belgrade where he grew plums for brandy. There had been a game of boules in the baking-hot sun and a press-up competition with their cousins. Peter had sunburned the back of his neck and his parents had worried about it. 'How ridiculous that seems now', says Robert, but Peter cuts across him to say, 'It was the best day ever', and Vikki adds, 'From the best day to the worst.'

Peter says he remembers walking down to the riverside in Belgrade the following day and waiting under a tree by the jet-ski club. 'That's literally the last thing I remember', he says. 'Honestly it's scary when I think back to it and then my mind literally goes blank. I don't remember anything after that. The next thing I knew I was in the ambulance from Leeds General Infirmary to Chapel Allerton Hospital.'

'That's two months later', says Robert and there is a moment of silence.

'Do you want me to tell it, Pete?' asks Vikki and Peter nods.

Vikki describes how Peter had almost backed out of going on the jet-ski but how she had talked him into it. 'That's my biggest regret', she says and then describes how they had set off with their instructors, how there had been a bang, but that she had thought nothing of it until her instructor had turned suddenly and made for a spot in the middle of the river.

'And I noticed a head, the body perpendicular to it in the water', says Vikki miming with an upright hand and her own head bowed at the neck. Peter murmurs, 'Face down.' 'So I just jumped in and lifted up this body and that's when I realised it was Pete, when I put his head up on my shoulder.' Vikki looks over at her little brother, who is following this intently, as though it is a story he has not heard before. 'And it looked like the river had been dyed red, just blood everywhere. I thought he was dead.'

Peter was conveyed by jet-ski to the shore and from there by ambulance to Belgrade Hospital, where a scan confirmed he had a bleed in the middle of his brain. Peter at this point scored just 3 in terms of responsiveness on the Glasgow Coma Scale. A severe head injury is anything below 9; below 5 survival rates are poor. The prognosis was bleak and ten days later, still largely unresponsive, Peter was flown home to Leeds General Infirmary. There the coma began to lift and little by little the long road of rehabilitation began. First Peter learned to walk again, 'like a new baby learning to walk, very unsteady on his feet', says Vikki. Next it was speech. 'That was eighteen days in', says Robert. 'The speech therapist got Peter to ring mum at work, didn't she? And he said, "Hi Mum, it's Peter."' 'Very robotic', says Vikki. The same week Peter was transferred to Chapel Allerton Hospital nearer home. 'And that's my very first memory,' says Peter. 'There were people all around me and I remember thinking *What's happened? Why am I here? Who are these people?* I remember clinging onto the rail in the ambulance because I honestly thought they were trying to kill me. I don't think I remembered I'd been in Serbia at all.'

After a few more weeks at the new hospital, Peter could now speak clearly and he could walk, but his siblings and parents knew that Peter was not at all himself. He made several attempts to escape.

'But gradually', says Peter, 'I began to gather my thoughts. I was still really shocked and coming to terms because I couldn't remember any of what they said had happened, so I was still not with it. But as I spent more time' – he pauses and looks at his father and his sister – 'you know, back in reality and I was speaking more and asking them questions, I started to understand what was happening to me.'

Not long before Christmas, he was discharged and eighteen months of outpatient rehabilitation followed. Everyone in the family, including Peter, thinks the rehabilitation period should have been longer, if only to help them come to terms with the metamorphosis Peter had undergone – in truth, the metamorphosis the whole family was undergoing.

'I knew that my personality had changed,' he says, tucking one socked foot underneath the other and looking at them, 'I realised literally the first day I went to school that January after my accident and I think my friends did too. I knew the way I was thinking and feeling, it wasn't' – he reaches for the word – 'right. Even though I did try and still am trying to be like I was before, everything had changed, everything.'

'Having seen the miracle of him coming back to life,' Robert says, 'maybe you delude yourself into thinking that you're going to return to something pre-accident. And in the early days it was difficult for me to accept and for the rest of the family to accept he's not the child that we used to have. It took probably two years before I fully realised that actually this was going to be a different Peter. It was still going to be a good Peter, but it was a different Peter.'

The family spend much of the rest of the morning discussing the finer points of that difference, as though trying to piece together so many shreds of paper scattered in a high wind. Each of the litany of differences they describe in the new Peter does not sound so very substantial in and of itself. Yet cumulatively you begin to realise how immense is the fall-out. It is the abrupt, involuntary break in continuity between past and present and the fact that this manifests at the granular level of personality that distinguishes Peter's story from the other fix-it-as-you-go-along changes in this book. It would seem to imply that we are, each of us, less a bundle of perceptions, as Hume would have it, than a confederation of small habits and quirks of thought and disposition that play out over time within our brains.

Peter is a little slower intellectually since the accident,

but also now obsessive about the minutiae of understanding. It takes him all day to read a chapter of a book, hours to watch a film on DVD, as he pauses every time he may have missed some vestige of meaning. That is part of a broader tendency to, as he says, 'over-think', which leads to anxiety, bouts of depression or sleeplessness and sometimes to rows, when some throwaway comment is replayed and replayed. He is more earnest about life in general and not always entirely realistic about what he can achieve. 'From being somebody fairly easy-going and fun-loving,' as his father puts it, 'now there's a tendency to want to save the world, isn't there?' Peter nods. 'You have grander ideas.'

They describe the plan Peter hatched last year to climb Annapurna. 'One of the highest mountains in the world', Peter says, bouncing on his chair for a moment. 'But are we allowed to mention Lady Gaga?' says Robert. 'Dad said he had more chance of shagging Lady Gaga than I had of getting up Annapurna.' All three of them laugh, although you catch in Peter's blue-grey eyes a faint look of bemusement that comes upon him from time to time in the course of the morning. It is like the expression of someone on the periphery of a conversation in a language they do not understand, but who nevertheless wishes to appear engaged. 'And he's put that on his board', says Robert. This is the whiteboard in Peter's orderly bedroom, where he writes down the things he does not want to forget, the date of his last haircut and what he asked the stylist to do, Dad's Annapurna quote, some training times for the Great North Run in which he competed a few months earlier and another quote that says in thick black marker, 'You haven't lost your sense of humour, Pete.' This is one of Peter's most nagging worries. He mentions at least half a dozen times during the conversation that he was more fun, more cool, before the accident. It weighs on him.

'I think a lot of my friends literally think it was just a

bang in the head, but it's so much more than that', says Peter. 'And sometimes I just feel like the head injury is doing a lot of the talking, not me. It's affected me in every way and you realise how important the way you think is to who you are. It's like a quest for me to make a new sense of my life and although I'm improving every day, I guess I'm still a work in progress.' And Peter shrugs and holds that blue-grey gaze for a long time.

Peter Holmes's twin brother, Alex, looks so like Peter that even their father cannot tell them apart in photographs. They were thought at birth to be fraternal twins, but everyone in the family suspects they are identical. According to Peter, they used even to think in the same way. 'There's no one who knows me inside out like him', he said. This magnified the toll of the accident for them both, along with the fact that the twins could no longer shadow each other in the way they always had. Alex was studying in Lisbon when the interview in Leeds took place, but some days later, on a crackly telephone line, he said this: 'Now I know how life can completely change in a few seconds and how you don't know how strong a relationship is until you've been through the worst. But what I've learned is that if you've got a loving enough family, then you can get through a really, really dark side of life, because although we've been a family as long as we've all been alive, we only ever saw the complete family dynamic after the accident. It's just made us very aware of how strong that familial love really is. And me and Pete, we're still really, really, really close. We still speak to each other every single day.'

　　Much of our intuitive thinking about how we love over time is predicated on some perceived stability of identity, however the world about us turns. Our long-standing affections can weather the onset of crow's feet, the gentle sagging and padding of the years, but still we tend to say of our partners, our families, our friends that What I Love About You Is ... [*complete as appropriate*].

The crux is that we fill in that space with what we see as stable qualities. Yet the Holmes family prove how flexible love can be in navigating a sudden and apparently fundamental change out there on the open sea of life. As his father said that morning, 'The thing is, I think we've all moved. Peter's a different person, but we've all become different people in the process.' Clearly this what-you-might-call 'limbic revision' has not been easy, heaven knows. It has taken a deliberate and sustained feat of imagination on all their parts and that work goes on. Yet in their resilience, humour and closeness they have afforded Peter a way to change. They have spun a thread of connection, a lifeline of story, between the old Peter, otherwise lost with that blow to the head, and the new Peter he is becoming, as the hundred billion nerve cells of his brain rewire. David Hume's 'fictitious' identity that may be, but in this case it seems worth believing in.

10

THE BODY

You may perhaps have been waiting for a change story like Mike Waudby's. And now here it is: an honest-to-goodness crowd-pleaser of a change, the kind that makes people whoop from the audience on daytime TV and total strangers click 'like' on Facebook. For Mike's metamorphosis lends itself well to the popular metric of Before and After shots, photographic proof of the extent to which an astonishing, and highly marketable, physical transformation is possible.

The Before looks like this: a morbidly obese man sits wedged into an armchair. It is hard to tell how old he is, the curves of his moon-face pushing his eyes into dark slits. He is wearing a vast black T-shirt, visibly sweaty at the armpits, and it has ridden up an inch or two at the front to reveal a slice of blue-pink belly. His thighs spill from the seat uncomfortably splayed and a fold of one forearm droops over the arm of the chair. The opposite hand is raised with middle finger aloft in the *doigt d'honneur*.

The After is much more uplifting. A buff young man in his early thirties leans casually on the arm of a chair. In his hands is one of those large plastic water bottles that people take to the gym and he is dressed in a grey V-neck tight enough to show off taut pectorals and sculpted biceps. His jaw is chiselled and in his big brown eyes there is just a glimmer of a smile. He looks like he could be advertising something, and in a way he is.

For Mike Waudby's extraordinary tale of redemption – 18 stone lost in eighteen months – is now what he hopes to build into a blockbusting weight-loss brand. There are herbal supplements, a personal training package, his ambition to compete as a professional bodybuilder. Not that any of these has exactly taken off yet; he is still 'skint', he says, but he is hopeful. But what is fascinating is the way in which the huge change Mike Waudby made in his life has become his *raison d'être*. He *is* the change at the moment, which may yet be an indication that the inner transformation is not over. Because, although the Mike who answers the door to a Victorian terraced house on a run-down street in Hull looks more or less like the confident hunk in the photos, he does not quite conduct himself like a confident hunk and leads the way inside a little gingerly, awkwardly, like he might be wearing someone else's skin.

Mike began to pile on weight towards the end of his teens. His first experience of heartbreak, a complicated home life and a long-standing struggle with depression were eased, he found, by getting drunk. Naturally shy by temperament and 'really unhappy', drinking gave him just the right combination of numbness and confidence. And the more he drank, the more he ate, until he could easily wash down an extra meal with two and half litres of cider or soak up a bottle of whisky with the late-night contents of the fridge.

'I didn't just drink. I drank to get drunk,' he says, sitting very straight on a dining chair he has pulled into the centre of the room, 'I had to drink more than everyone else, and if

I had something to eat, it was big.' He pauses and, gesturing as if holding a very large plate, he says it again. 'Big.'

Mike hit 21 stone just before his twenty-first birthday and gradually he began to feel the pariah status our society so often assigns the overweight. Sensitive at the best of times, he became keenly aware of every slight: the couple walking hand-in-hand who would look at him and exchange glances or shake their heads, the cashiers in shops who would whisper and titter the moment he was out of earshot.

'Even though I was always polite,' he says, 'and I never did anything to harm anyone, society really hated me and I felt, like, why? Only because of the way I look. I wasn't even that heavy at this point.'

It was Tolstoy who maintained that 'Our body is a machine for living', but Mike's was becoming a machine that increasingly got in the way of living, or at least of normal living. The cascade of perceived stigma became mortifying, the tipping-point an unpleasant episode that now set the tone for the rest of his twenties.

'I was sat in a local bar with my friend Andy,' he says, with a slight gesture of his head toward the street outside, 'and this girl just walked up to me and she says, "Do you mind leaving the bar?" I was quite confused. I says, "Why?" and she went, "Because you're making us all feel sick." And a whole group of tables started laughing. She didn't. She looked me stern in the face and said, "I want you to leave." And then what was more humiliating was that the bar staff and some group of blokes all started laughing and staring at me, and Andy went, "Come on, let's just go." So we left and she said some stuff on the way out. "Yeah, go away fat boy." And then when I went to get in the taxi to go home, he wouldn't let me in. He just went, "You're too fat, you'll ruin my suspension." So after that, I took the easy option. I thought, *OK, I'm not going out any more.'*

For the next seven years Mike Waudby sat at home in his parents' house and that was it, until he became a bona fide recluse. He had been put on sick benefit by his doctor because of depression, so there was no need to get to the Job Centre. He had his drink delivered direct, ate the food his mother cooked and as the years passed, he grew, in his words, 'bigger and bigger and bigger'. His mother worried, his father shouted, his sisters teased, but Mike stayed put in his bedroom, churning over all the things he should have said to the assorted people who were to blame for all this. '*What are you staring at? What's your problem?* Over and over, and then I'd start drinking and everything would seem fine, like it'll fix itself.'

Carefully, Mike now walks upstairs, light on his socked feet, to show the large, dim Victorian bedroom that was his prison. He runs his fingers over a fist-sized dent in the wood-chip wallpaper where he punched the wall in a moment of frustration and rage. There is the desk with its computer, a few pens in pots, some DVDs and a super-sized office chair. Here he says he would watch TV, browse the internet, chat to girls on MySpace and try to ignore his increasing physical discomfort, the pressure points, the sores, the shooting pains in his fingers and his feet that came from cramming himself into chairs not designed to support a man of his size, the acid burn in his throat from the booze.

By twenty-seven, Mike was 'in so much pain mentally and physically' that he decided to go to the doctor. 'My little cry for help it was,' says Mike, 'and it was a terrifying experience.' His father had to unbolt the front seat of the car so that Mike could get in and in the waiting-room everyone stared. The doctor weighed him – 33 stone – and told him to stop drinking, try eating cereal before he went to bed and pre-scribed a course of anti-depressants. Some days later, Mike gathered every pill he could find in the house – paracetamol, valium – sat down at his desk and washed them down with an eight-pack of lager and two bottles of scotch.

'It's the same desk', he says, reaching out to touch it. 'I just popped as many tablets as I could. I put my favourite album on, Guns N' Roses, *Appetite for Destruction*, and I was just listening to that, looking at a blank screen thinking, I've finally done it. I've finally had the balls to do this. The next thing I knew, I woke up at the desk, no hangover, no pains, no nothing, and I realised that I was still here in this humungous body.'

It was a sickening moment, but something strange began to happen in the days that followed. Mike's need for alcohol fell away and he began to wonder why he had survived. Struck by some kind of secular epiphany, he was all of a sudden engulfed by a sense of responsibility for having got himself to this terrible place and an entirely novel sense of agency that only he could get himself out.

'It's hard to explain but it just sort of happened', says Mike. 'And it was regret more than anything, this sudden realisation when I stopped saying to myself *Poor you, it's not your fault* and I went *You absolute idiot, it's all your fault*. It dawned on me that I don't need doctors or anyone else to lose weight. I was going to have to do something myself because I wanted my life back. I wanted to step outside that front door you came in and I wanted to go to the shop or go to a bar. I wanted to get in my car and to go to work, I wanted to be someone's best friend. I wanted to be some-one's world, because all the things that life has, I couldn't do.' Mike pauses for a moment, his fists clenched on his lap. 'I wanted to live a life.'

So Mike set about making his body 'a machine for living'. He talked to his dad, who did not shout this time, but spent his last £450 on a mail-order cross trainer, which he set up in Mike's bedroom. It was a cheap one, only designed to take up 21 stone in weight, but the next morning Mike got out of bed and clambered on. What seemed to him 'like an eternity' passed. He looked down, gasping for breath: two minutes. But that evening Mike did not have a drink or any junk food 'and that's when it all started,' he says. 'I became the most driven person.'

While endless permutations crowd the self-help shelves, in reality the formula for losing weight is no particular mystery: eat less, exercise more. But for someone in Mike's position, this presented a change akin to a smooth vertical surface to be scaled without ropes or safety gear, the most psychologically intimidating of goals. The only way Mike seems to have found a foothold was to take it step by step, in a harness of existing character traits now turned to the new purpose: a tendency to extremes, a proclivity for self-punishment and an intensely habitual nature. He chose what to change and he changed it. With no outside intervention whatsoever, without so much as browsing weight-loss plans online, Mike constructed a punishing routine for himself. He stopped drinking altogether. He confined himself to a rigid diet of his own making, the same three 'bland, boring' meals eaten at the appointed hour like clockwork and three sessions on the cross trainer, which built up in a matter of weeks to 180 minutes of gruelling daily exercise.

'The chaffing was horrendous, just raw red skin, and my feet used to go numb. I didn't care about that kind of pain, but those sessions were the most mentally painful experience I could ever go back and relive.' He says this quietly, 'My head, my mind, realising what I'd done. So a lot of that motivation was anger at myself for what had happened. But I knew if I give up now, I'll never do it. '

There is a knock at the door and Mike's mum comes in with a plate of food, an omelette, some cold chicken, a heap of watery-looking salad. Mike glances at his watch.

'Is it OK if I have something to eat?' he says. 'I'm still quite fixated on my diet.' He smiles and begins to eat in silence.

We often reflexively talk about the adult brain as though it were fixed, but of course, thanks to much-vaunted advances in brain science over the last half-century, many people have at least heard of neuroplasticity. That is the name given to the changes that happen in our brains as our lives change in small or large ways. Quietly, neuroplasticity hums away within every story you will read in this book.

There is the sometimes dramatic plasticity that occurs in response to injury, as for Peter Holmes, but there is also the plasticity of Peter's family, that of neural pathways and synapses associated with changes in behaviour, emotions, thought processes or environment. We can imagine – within our own plastic brains – the shifting maps of connection in the heads of the two Alinas as they rehearsed the magic trick of their new signatures, in Shander Herian's as his sight returned, or in Joanne Fleisher's when she fell in love with Judy. And beneath the cranium of Mike Waudby as he toiled on his cross trainer, ate his lean meals on time, picture the veritable maze of new byways.

There remains the chicken-and-egg question of whether the changed brain changes us, or whether we change and our brains then follow. We shall leave first causes to the scientists, but the fact is that our brains are doing this all our lives. Plasticity is part of us at the most fundamental level, even, as a number of recent studies have shown, into old age. Like Heraclitus' river, this form of change is who we are. And for anyone doubtful of the extent to which we can change, neuroplasticity provides the knockdown argument.

Neuroplasticity gained ascendancy as an idea in the 1960s and '70s, hitting the popular science vernacular towards the millennium. The concept was in fact mooted on the scientific fringes – and mostly ignored – as early as the 1790s, when a Piedmontese anatomist noted differences in the dissected brains of trained and untrained dogs. Another oft-overlooked reference comes within a short treatise written in the 1880s by our old bewhiskered friend the philosopher, William James. *Habit* offers sixty-eight slender pages of reflection on the relationship between what we do and who we are. And it suggests a course of action for when the who-we-are gets fed up with the what-we-do.

James opens with a statement that again carries an echo of David Hume: 'When we look at living creatures ... one of the first things that strike us is that they are bundles of habits.' He goes on to argue that these habits are the very building blocks of human change because of 'plasticity' and its combination of continuity and transformation:

> Plasticity then in the wide sense of the word means the possession of a structure weak enough to yield to an influence, but strong enough not to yield all at once. ... Organic matter, especially nervous tissue, seems endowed with a very extraordinary degree of plasticity of this sort; so that we may without hesitation lay down our first proposition ... that the phenomena of habit in living beings are due to the plasticity of the organic materials of which their bodies are composed.

There follows a discussion of how habits – from putting our hands in our pockets or biting our nails to weightier dispositional idiosyncrasies – 'deepen old paths or make new ones' in our brains. Where James goes wrong is to assert that this brain plasticity is a feature of youth and that by the age of thirty 'the character has set like plaster, never to soften again'. This idea of plasticity as a function of juvenility hung about in neuroscience until it was overturned in the late twentieth century. But James makes it his impetus for a call to get your habitual house in order before it is too late and he offers some handy advice about how to do so. One must launch oneself at the habit-breaking initiative in as decisive and expeditious a manner as possible. There must be no slip-ups and one must furthermore make a daily habit of reaching beyond one's comfort zone, so as to be better equipped to handle future habit-busting changes. 'The hell to be endured hereafter', James finally booms from the page, 'is no worse than the hell we make for ourselves in this world by habitually fashioning our characters the wrong way. We are spinning our own fates.' William James might well have written his treatise with Mike Waudby in mind.

There is one habit Mike has yet to break, one persistent neural pathway as yet undisturbed. He says that he still tends to pull up the waistband of his trousers or sit with a cushion in his lap to mask a large belly that is no longer there. Today it is the cushion. He has been leaning on it to eat his lunch, but there it remains long after he has set aside his empty plate.

He has been describing how his routine, his new set of habits, steeled his resolve against pizzas and lager through those early days when he would heave himself off the cross trainer, look at his body and weep. 'But no matter how many times I felt like crap, I knew what I had to do. I knew what I had to eat and I knew I had to train. Without that routine, I wouldn't have been able to pick myself up.' Just as William James wrote.

After about eight weeks of this regime, Mike felt his T-shirt getting baggier and it was at this point that he realised he needed to weigh himself again. But when you are heavier than a family of four, weighing yourself is no easy matter. Again his father unbolted the seat of his car and they drove around Hull looking for a chemist with a set of old-fashioned heavy-duty scales. They then sat outside until Mike plucked up the courage to go in.

'I didn't look at anyone,' says Mike, his fingers gripping the fabric of the cushion, 'I kept my head down. The scales were right at the back of the store and I got on. This group of women came up behind me to look at some shampoo or something and I put my money in, thinking it would just show my weight and give me a receipt. But oh no, it had to speak full-blast in an electronic voice. "You Are About To Be Weighed, Please Remain Still And Look Straight." The whole shop had taken notice. I'm shaking with fear. And then it says, "You Weigh 29 Stone 13 Pounds." I'm like, *You told the entire shop*. So I took my receipt, got in the car and I started crying. But what I'd got was this ticket, so I began to think, *OK, I've lost three stone. Great*.'

That was 15 May 2009. Mike sold a couple of old games consoles and bought himself some second-hand gym weights to celebrate. Over the next fifteen months he and his father went to that chemist every two weeks: 28 stone 2, 27 stone 8, 26 stone 4, 25 stone, 24 stone, 23 stone, 22 stone, 21 stone. About a year into the weight loss, things plateaued for a week or two, so Mike signed up to a backstreet gym and from there, as he says, 'Boom!' 20 stone, 19, 18, 17, 16 and finally, at 10.35 a.m. on 9 August 2010, 'You Weigh 15 Stone 7 Pounds.' After that, Mike went to the gym to weigh himself until he finally reached the optimal weight for his height and build, 14 stone 7, just as the leaves of 2010 were turning from green to autumnal orange.

The only problem now was that the chrysalis of his metamorphosis, the skin that had held that 33-stone man, now hung about Mike's form like loose upholstery. As people on all sides congratulated him, Mike felt, he says, 'as ugly as I did when I was 33 stone, because all this time, I wanted a relationship and I thought *how can a girl like this?* I suppose it's vanity in that sense.' That winter his dad took out a loan to pay for the cosmetic removal of some of his loose skin. Mike then began to work out to fill the rest with muscle.

Thus a beautiful butterfly, albeit a brawny one, emerged at last into the world and finally, *finally*, the emphasis shifted from regret to ambition, from burning platform to shining beacon. Over the eighteen months that followed Mike found love, he qualified as a personal trainer and soon started his weight-loss business, along with a sideline in renovating furniture and motor bikes. Life began. But this was no substitution trunk trick. Mike made an extraordinary outward change and only then could the door be opened to an inner transformation that is still clearly under way.

'I think the inner Mike,' he says, carefully picking up the cushion from his lap and placing it on the floor, 'that 33-stone guy who was a recluse, will never leave me. He'll always be there. But I'm getting better at beating him every single day and I feel better in myself, you know? I've still got a way to go in loving myself. But then I'll get up in the morning and I'll remember getting out of this bed at 30 stone, then at 28 stone, then at 26 stone and I never stopped. I'm not going to fucking stop now. I need something to chase, something to fight for. It's what keeps me going. And now this is my chance to make a career inspiring others that if I can do it, then so can you.'

And he is right. If Mike can do it, then so can you. He built himself 'a machine for living', a machine for showing the extent to which people can change and that they do.

PART III

HOW DO WE CHANGE?

11

THE SOUL AS BUTTERFLY

After the damp chill of January in the north of England, April in Paris is a blessed relief. The turning world has tilted on its axis and winter given way to spring. From the airport train, a collapsed warehouse by the tracks, its graffitied walls crumpled, steel frame like the picked bones of a carcass, now cloisters a little garden of new life. A cheerful tangle of flowering weeds nod their heads in the sunshine. A cloud of butterflies plays about a clump of buddleia, fluttering a greeting at the passing commuters bound for the orderly splendour of the 1st *arrondissement*. There, beyond the station, boulevards of horse chestnuts are in blossom, their floral candles pert and fresh. Passing one of the great iron paws of Gustave Eiffel's tower on your own more modest feet and glancing up into a sky of brightest blue, it is not hard to feel hopeful of new beginnings. It is one of those days that nourish the soul.

In ancient Greek the word for soul and for butterfly, that tiny maestro of change, is one and the same: ψυχή, *psyche*. The etymology of our own word 'butterfly' is somewhat disappointing by comparison. Its origins are debated, but one celebrated etymologist (a cousin of Charles Darwin) conjectured that it comes from the old Dutch *boterschijte*, referring to the buttery colour of the insect's excrement. But let us go with soul rather than shit for the time being and begin to consider not why or whether but *how* a soul – or a psyche – can change, yes even like a butterfly.

One answer to that question lies a short walk on this perfect spring day down the road from the Eiffel Tower. There, behind a pair of tall classical doors, is an office, warm and unexpectedly modern, and within the office is Didier Long, also warm and, when you know his story, unexpectedly modern. Because Didier Long knows a thing or two about how we change – he has done it more than most. Indeed Didier's soul has been on a veritable odyssey to bring him here today.

Thirty years ago Didier Long was a novice Benedictine monk at the austere Abbaye Sainte-Marie de la Pierre-Qui-Vire, buried deep in the vast Morvan forest of Burgundy. He was just nineteen when he joined the monastery and within six months he had taken the community's silent rule, shaved his head, sloughed off his old name and donned the habit – for religious clothes wear that name too – of Frère Marc.

This was the first great change in Didier's life. Only a few years earlier he had been a particularly difficult teenager, the black sheep of two identical twins who grew up in the industrial town of Clermont-Ferrand. 'I was delinquent,' Didier says, adjusting his glasses with scholarly animation, 'a petty thug, I was already stealing mopeds at thirteen. I think I was afraid deep down and couldn't get rid of that fear, so I became violent – extremely violent in the end.' He describes knocking two bloody teeth from a man almost twice his modest height who had casually insulted him on a beach. He talks about the cut-throat razor he carried wherever he went. He mentions his girlfriend at sixteen and how they just 'fucked all the time, because I didn't have the words to communicate. I did everything you can do to her', he says and winces slightly. He adds, almost as an afterthought, that not long before his seventeenth birthday he tried to take his own life. Didier says this in a matter-of-fact way, his sparkly eyes undimmed and with no further explanation other than that 'I didn't really see what the point of my life was.'

It was in the months after he came out of hospital during the autumn of 1983 that Didier experienced what could only be described as a revelation. This is the mysterious first part of how change often comes about. He had gone to convalesce at the country home of a friend. The boy's father was a professor of medieval theology from the university in town, a tough but learned figure who would tolerate no temper tantrums or bed-hopping. When he caught Didier sleeping with his niece, he curtly said, 'Didier, my house is not a brothel' and left it at that. But he listened to the young man's woes, read the Bible to him, lit candles for his soul.

'And suddenly' – Didier leans urgently across the black Formica table-top to make this point – 'I experienced some sort of upheaval. Not because of the Bible. I don't know why, I still don't. But suddenly I realised that the world wasn't how I'd pictured it up until then. There was a kind of depth to it. My suicide attempt had happened in the autumn and now spring came, the birds were singing, there was light and I thought *I'm alive*. And I saw that life was wonderful, as if things shone from the inside and the world around me was full of an energy that I'd never understood before.' He leans back and looks for a moment at a bird wheeling in the air outside the window. 'Of course, I understood that it was God, this mysterious force which inhabited everything, and

that this force loved me. And that feeling has never left me.'
He smiles as though he has just been handed a present. 'It
changed my life entirely and I thought I'm going to give my
life to that. It seemed like the least I could do.' And there
follows a little volley of laughter.

In a striking parallel to the experience of Mike Waudby,
Didier now turned his long-held tendency to extremes
towards religious devotion in lieu of fighting and sex. 'I
couldn't even imagine doing things half-heartedly', he says,
and he wrote to the Abbot at Pierre-Qui-Vire to arrange a
visit. He describes his first journey to the monastery through
what seemed like hours of dark forest, then a great stone
citadel of light, its soaring arches and, within, a hundred
black-clad monks in crystalline silence. A year later, Didier
Long was one of them.

Monastic life was severe. The monks rise at 2 a.m. There
are seven holy offices a day and, especially as a novice, you do
as you are told: you follow the rule, you undertake hard, physical work, all burden of choice lifted from your shoulders and
replaced with a new yoke of service to God. As Didier says,
it is 'as if everything that happened before did not exist'. The
former aristocrat sits at the same table as the would-be teenage
suicide. Everyone is equal. Everybody starts again. You have
a new name and you learn a new way of walking, standing,
sitting, singing, kneeling, even a new way of breathing. You
never eat meat, never drink wine. You are schooled in the
spare sign language of the silent order. Didier demonstrates
with a few gestures far more muted than his own. 'I'd like to
speak with you.' 'Father Abbot.' 'The dish.' 'Afterwards.' 'Let's
work.' There is a parlour where you can request an audience
with another monk, the sides of the conversation transmit-
ted by notes placed in a box called a 'babillard' (ironically the
French for 'babbler'), but according to Didier, they did not
have much need of it. Silence was good.

Didier explains the hardships in great detail, but he is at pains to point out that, while the beds were hard, the abbey cold, the work arduous, the life highly circumscribed, these sundry constraints nevertheless offer a gateway to a very individual 'inner journey'. The map of this journey he sketches out on the shiny black table in little fingerprints and smears of gesture. At one point, 'Who You Are', 'What You Do' and 'What You Believe' linger in a faint Venn diagram there. And gradually it becomes clear that this inner journey, as much as any blinding flash of divine revelation, is where the true metamorphosis takes place; this is how the soul is transformed.

'And you don't know what you're going to become,' he says, 'because monastic life is an exercise. It isn't faith. They don't ask you what you believe. They don't care. It's about whether you are in service or not. You go from despair to joy, or you feel very close to God one day and the next you don't, and you go through all these feelings in silence. So the monastery is' – Didier pauses to think for a long time – 'it's a mirror to the soul. Your soul is in front of you. You watch it evolve. And there's no greater adventure than that.'

The one time the spoken word was permitted at Pierre-Qui-Vire was during lessons, for in tandem with great austerity ran the monastery's exuberant intellectual life. To become a man of God, your thinking gear had also to be in service and for Didier this was 'a profound change'. Reborn as an intellectual, he now learned Hebrew, Latin, Greek, theology, psychology, philosophy, painting.

'People think the lack of sex is the hardest thing,' he says, anticipating the next question, 'but it's not. You redirect your whole psyche and your body becomes a tool. For God. There's a lot of mental and physical work and all of that changes your relationship to desire, because nothing moves, only the seasons change. So in a way you lock yourself up in order to become free.' And Didier gets up to open the tall casement window.

After the candid account of his years as a teenage libertine, the conviction with which Didier describes his secluded vocation comes as something of a surprise, not least because, self-evidently, he is no longer Frère Marc. Here we are at a boardroom table in a boutique internet consultancy in central Paris speaking with the managing director in his pressed white shirt, a little tight about the neck, his slim blue tie knotted like a schoolboy's. Nothing quite fits any preconception with which one might have walked into the room: either the knife-carrying delinquent or the monk or the metropolitan businessman. Such is Didier's natural volubility that many years of silence would seem a feat indeed. His two dark, impish eyes dance as he talks, whether of teenage rutting or of holy asceticism. Through the open window the sounds of the world now leak in, children playing in a nearby yard, the howl of an ambulance, a flurry of laughter from two passing pedestrians.

Yet ask Didier whether he ever missed the world during those years deep in the forest of his soul at Pierre-Qui-Vire and he says 'no' three times in quick succession. 'I'd suffered too much in the world to want to go back.'

'So you were happy?'

'Yes,' he says, 'It's a beautiful life, monastic life. I was very happy. It's the opposite of what people think. It's a real community. There's genuine affection between monks. When I was there, there was a former Waffen SS officer who'd lost an eye defending Hitler in Berlin and there was another monk who'd been part of the Resistance. He'd blocked Hitler's tanks in Normandy. And now these men were together. Wars produce monks actually. I think, faced with the absurdity of the world, God had been their answer. For me too, God was the answer to the void. So it's a life in which you share all of that and monks are happy people, very loving. There are no masks in a monastery, nothing to hide behind. So you love each other, and it works well. It never crossed my mind that I'd want to leave.'

But in May 1995, a decade into Didier's life as Frère Marc, something extraordinary happened. Now editor of Pierre-Qui-Vire's small imprint of theological books, Didier was overseeing the production of their first CD-ROMs. This was cutting-edge technology at the time and, in a community still imagined by the outside world to be stooped with quill and ink in the scriptorium, the project made an appealing news story. So the TV channel France 2 sent along a news crew whom the Abbot asked Frère Marc to escort. The producer was a woman called Marie-Pierre Samitier and the moment she walked into Didier's office, he fell in love.

'I saw this woman come in and I thought, *This is my wife. God has sent her to me.* I instantly understood she was the love of my life. I didn't know anything about her. I just knew she was effervescent, full of life, and she threw me off balance. She threw me.' Didier smiles at the incongruity of this. 'And it was a very, very, very deep conviction. Just as when I entered the monastery, I was deeply convinced. The thing is you don't change reasonably, rationally. I think we change because we are called, something or someone calls you. It's a feeling and then you rationalise it. It's like belief. You believe something and then you do what you believe. You don't believe what you do. You do what you believe.'

Didier pauses for a moment, almost as though his own insight has taken him by surprise. And it is a remarkable truth about how we change, well worth holding on to, that the 'how' of change lives in that combination of belief and action, of intuition and agency. It is a process that is simultaneously mystical and pragmatic.

None the wiser, Marie-Pierre Samitier left the monastery

the following day, but the world had turned. This was not by any means the first woman Didier had encountered in his years at the monastery, nor was it the first time a monk there had fallen in love. Indeed there was an established protocol for what to do if one's vocation was so rudely interrupted by desire, but Frère Marc side-stepped it. He went straight to the abbot and said that he was no longer cut out for the monastic life. 'I chose' is how Didier puts it and he would bide no objection, no plea to wait for a year and see whether his equilibrium would be restored.

Three months later, just four days before Didier's younger brother was due to collect him from the monastery and return him to the world, Marie-Pierre Samitier contacted him out of the blue and asked to come and speak with him. He agreed and she arrived the next day. Clearly, she had also felt some kind of connection, for she now unburdened herself about her failing marriage, the husband who had left her and their two young children. The first rule of St Benedict is to listen without prejudice, so Didier gently stopped her and warned Marie-Pierre that he was not neutral. 'Why?' she had asked. 'Because I'm in love with you' came the reply. But Marie-Pierre did not return his affections and she said that he was 'crazy' to consider leaving the monastery. 'What are you going to do?' she had asked, 'you'll be completely crushed. The world is a dangerous place.' And with that, she had hastily left.

'I'd hoped she'd be in love with me,' says Didier, 'but it didn't matter. If God calls me elsewhere, he calls me elsewhere. That was the Wednesday and on Saturday I left Pierre-Qui-Vire with my younger brother. What's odd is that it was a beautiful day and the forest was filled with light – the oaks, the water, the animals. We stopped to eat among the trees and I remember thinking it was like leaving paradise in a way and I didn't know where I was going.'

Way back into antiquity people have been divided as to whether, in an ideal world, it is better to change course or to stick to your guns, whether strength lies in the steadfast oak or the flexible reed, as Aesop framed it.

This was the way the conversation turned late one evening in Athens a couple of centuries after Aesop, sometime in the mid-fourth century BC. Two of Plato's elder brothers, so the philosopher reports, were at a small after-party following the night-time festival of the goddess Bendis, with its thrilling torch relay on horseback and other diversions. Plato's brothers were serious-minded fellows – you get these people at parties – and as others lounged and discussed the festivities, they found themselves shooting the breeze with their tutor, Socrates. A disquisition followed on the nature of justice, beauty, education, evil, what the Gods think about and – to our theme – whether they change. In truth it was a somewhat one-sided discussion, which also happens at parties, with Socrates holding forth, his two students merely punctuating with a helpful 'of course', a 'very true' or an 'undoubtedly' here or there. According to Socrates' way of thinking, which differs from Aesop, 'things which are at their best are also least liable to be altered'. The principle applies, said he, to furniture, houses and clothes, but also to the 'bravest and wisest souls' which are 'least confused or deranged by any external influence'.

Yet away from Mount Olympus and far from Platonic ideals, the very reverse frequently turns out to be true. Indeed alteration of the soul in the welter of a mortal life is often the very fruit of courage and of growing wisdom, as the tale of Didier Long quietly shows. With a lovely echo of Plato's revisionist student Aristotle, the American psychologist and pioneer of humanistic psychotherapy Carl Rogers put it like this in his 1961 book about change, *Becoming a Person*: 'This process of the good life is not, I am convinced, a life for the faint-hearted. It involves the stretching and growing of becoming more and more of one's potentialities. It involves the courage to be. It means launching oneself fully into the stream of life.'

So picture the former monk arriving in Paris in the autumn of 1995 and duly launching himself into the stream of life. With clothes fifteen years out of date, just 20,000 francs (around £2,000) in cash in his pocket, no bank account, no job, no home, no friends, Didier nonetheless had a sense of 'huge energy inside me'. Within three weeks he had a job producing CD-ROMs about the Bible and medieval history. He rented a tiny flat and filled it with as much Ikea furniture as his remaining francs would buy. 'The guys in the office called me ET, but I was Robinson Crusoe', he says and he cackles.

Then, one evening, the phone rang and it was Marie-Pierre. She said she felt guilty about his decision to leave the monastery and had rung every 'Long' in the phone book to find out if they had a relative called Frère Marc who used to be at Pierre-Qui-Vire. She invited him to lunch to make amends and Didier arrived in a flowery shirt from the early '80s and promptly ordered everything on the menu. He roars with laughter; 'you don't eat much in monasteries!' Little by little, over the months that followed, Marie-Pierre now fell in love with Didier, finding amid the rancour of her divorce an eccentric little island of happiness and humour in this 'Charlie Chaplin' figure, as Didier calls himself, coming to terms with the modern world. 'I made her laugh and that laughter cured us.'

A year later Didier bought the house that Marie-Pierre

was struggling to repay, moved in and became father to her children. A year after that they were married and remain inseparable to this day. 'Souls find each other,' he says, 'I think that's how it is.'

Didier's career now took off, for if there was one thing he had learned at Pierre-Qui-Vire it was how to learn, and fast. Soon he had built a number of high-profile retail web sites and was recruited to McKinsey, Colin Price's old consultancy, as an internet adviser. Didier was not, perhaps unsurprisingly, a company man. 'I'm too radical,' he says, 'I bang my fist on the table when I hear a lie.' So, some six years after his arrival in Paris, Didier set up his own now very successful technology consultancy. He is, he says, 'a monk in business, not a businessman, but a business monk'. And he rolls about with laughter.

For, as Didier says, once a monk always a monk, but the problem with making changes as huge as those he has made, where whole worlds are swapped like playing cards, is that you risk becoming fragmented to the point of madness. 'So you need a centre', says Didier and for him that centre has remained the Bible 'as a kind of instruction manual, an explanation of life'. This is what has helped him manage the moments of doubt, such as the occasion a colleague from McKinsey visited Pierre-Qui-Vire and returned saying that they had hoped Frère Marc would become abbot one day, a great spiritual man. He shrugs and says, 'Any choice necessarily implies nostalgia for what you haven't chosen, but life' – Didier smoothes both palms across the table-top – 'is not behind you. It's not even in front. It's here right now. And what is going on here right now is more important than anything that could have happened.'

In that vivid present Didier Long still had one more great change ahead of him. His soul had not made its final metamorphosis to butterfly quite yet.

In the years after leaving Pierre-Qui-Vire, Didier had struggled to find a religious observance he felt comfortable with. He would have no truck with 'the idiots with guitars' and increasingly his ongoing private theological studies – for this was still how he spent his evenings after work – focused on an increasing fascination with the Jewishness of Jesus. When he prayed, these days, he often did so in Hebrew and friends cracked jokes about how he was no longer really Christian.

Then, on the first day of 2010, came a devastating blow. Didier's best friend in Paris, a man with whom he had worked in the late 1990s, died in an avalanche in the Alps. It was Didier who drove to Les Arcs to identify his body. When the town authorities said that the ground was too hard to dig a grave, it was he who told them he had dug thirty graves in the frozen ground at the abbey and that he would do so now, if someone might fetch him a pickaxe. When he rose to recite the psalm at the grave he had just dug, the words came to him in Hebrew and that is the moment that the former delinquent-cum-Benedictine-monk-cum-businessman decided, as he says, 'that I am Jewish'.

From that day Didier wore the kippah (skullcap), observed Shabbat and read the Talmud. By the autumn he spent every Saturday morning at the orthodox synagogue at the end of his street and over the next year he delved into his own lineage and into that of Marie-Pierre, discovering their mutual Jewish ancestry. She had never been religious in any way, but now they made this journey of the soul together. 'If she hadn't changed, I might not have either,' says Didier, 'and it's wonderful. I feel I'm diving into an ocean.' And he runs the pad of his thumb over a thick gold ring with Hebrew words around it.

If you attempt to speak of 'conversion' with Didier, he resists. While his testimony is punctuated with defining moments, the man himself defies definition, repeating that his experience speaks less of overnight transformation than of the journey a soul takes in the course of a life.

'So in a way I don't feel that I've changed lives. I feel I've simply become myself. Via the monastery, via Marie-Pierre, via discovering that we are Jewish. There are changes, of course. When I wear my hat or my kippah or carry my Talmud, someone who sees that and recalls the monk tends to feel it's not the same person. But I don't see it like that. I'm still Didier and I'm still Frère Marc. Spirituality isn't something outside us. It's life; it's experience and it's in *this* world that it's happening. It's us who are acting. There's no miracles. We are the ones who decide and there are many ways of living. But it's not four lives or three lives or two lives. It's one life.' Didier draws a fingertip across the table. 'God writes straight with curved lines, but it is one life. From my birth until now. So people say Didier is a spiritual adventurer and it's true. I am.'

The psychological study of religious conversion has chiefly (although not exclusively) focused on the American Protestant experience, yielding various not entirely surprising models of how this particular vein of change takes place. Often the spotlight has fallen on experiences that seem to mirror the sudden spiritual paroxysm of Paul on the road to what these days is war-torn Damascus. Or there are the seven stages of the Rambo model (not Sylvester Stallone but a US theological seminary professor) that plot an orderly course for the spiritually hungry from crisis through quest and commitment to new identity. As this book now turns to explore how people change, there will be more of these step models. They often read like driving instructions from Google Maps.

And so at every bend in the road we would do well to recollect Didier's notion of the soul as adventurer on a long and – this is important – *uncharted* voyage. A soul that is free like a butterfly.

Asked if he anticipates making further great life changes, Didier Long is silent for a long time and then says this: 'It's impossible to answer that. Because who would have thought one day I'd be a monk? Who'd have thought I'd meet a woman? Who'd have thought I'd become Jewish? It was impossible, even for me, to imagine. So maybe there'll be other great changes in my life, I don't know. It's impossible to know.' He grins and in the black dots of his eyes you can almost see the fluttering of wings.

12

ON BROTHERHOOD

Five years and a week after Didier Long began a new chapter of his life as a Jewish man in Paris, three gunmen claiming affiliation to the group calling itself Al-Qaeda in the Arabian Peninsula carried out a spate of shootings across the city. Twelve died at the offices of the satirical newspaper *Charlie Hebdo*, a police officer was shot dead at a traffic junction across town and another four perished in the siege at a Jewish supermarket in Porte de Vincennes. The three gunmen, also killed, were all French citizens.

When asked that day at his office – just a few months after the attacks – whether all this felt somehow closer to home now that he was Jewish, Didier smiled. He said that it was a very interesting question, before apparently answering a rather different one. What he said seems now to prefigure what happened on the streets of Paris six months later.

'What I think,' he said, 'is that these terrorists are people who've lost all consideration for themselves, people who are empty, who don't feel they exist. So suddenly someone tells them, "You will finally exist, briefly, like a shooting star, and spirituality can offer this." So they think that in the terrorist act, they'll finally live. So I think it's a manipulation, the opposite of spiritual.' Didier had paused and then said, 'Could I have become a terrorist? It's something I've often wondered. Because I was nothing, I was empty and suddenly God called me and I went to a monastery, but I could very well have gone to a madrasa and ended up in the World Trade Center. The difference is that I met people who built me.'

The clanging of metal chairs being stacked, the pop of pool shots and the hum of a drinks machine all seep through into a windowless back office at a youth centre in Walthamstow, north-east London. Here a conversation of some intensity is unfolding beneath a single strip light.

'Would you view yourself as having been radicalised?'

'No, not really, but I guess from the outside looking in, you'd think I had.'

'I mean, you *had* been radicalised, hadn't you? You'd certainly set off down the road.'

'I'd like to say no, though the reality is that, yes, I had. But look, this is where a lot of people get it all wrong. I'd say I was abused. My emotions were abused, my sympathies, my faith, you know? It was a strategy of manipulating what I felt and how I felt to suit their own objectives. And I wasn't a kid, so I was stupid for believing it, but it was the praying, them being so devout. I was fooled into thinking that these are really pious individuals and that they wouldn't lie. So it was naive, I'd say. And there's this bond of brotherhood, it's embedded within Islam, so here was a route for me to do something about the innocent people being killed. I felt that I had a role to play and I do, but just not that way.'

'Would you have been prepared to take up arms if it had come to that?'

'Yes, I think it would've ended up in that situation. I really don't know what was planned for me, but it scares the life out of me to be honest. Looking back now, it did change me from being who I am. I lost my identity, to tell the truth, at that point.'

And Hanif Qadir sighs deeply, swivelling his bulk back and forth on the tatty office chair for a moment. There is a knock and a young man in sports gear and a white *taqiyah* pops his head around the door, a stack of chairs in hand.

'Mind if I leave these in here, Han?'

'Yeah, you're alright, mate', says Hanif and his grizzled features erupt into a smile.

Hanif Qadir grew up in a small town on Teesside, one of five children and three inseparable brothers. His father had arrived from Pakistan-administered Kashmir in the 1950s, but Hanif has no recollection of ever feeling like they were immigrants back then. This was home and his was an idyllic childhood on their little street of fifteen houses. There was Auntie Connie and Uncle Dick next door, who were like a real aunt and uncle to seven-year-old Hanif when his father died. There was Mrs Braithwaite opposite, who would cram all the children into her kitchen at Easter time to paint eggs. Hanif remembers helping to ring the church bells one Christmas and that their neighbours would also celebrate the Qadirs' religious holidays with them. Uncle Dick would always shovel the snow from their front drive in winter and when Hanif and his brothers were bigger, they did the same for the whole street. 'It was a beautiful childhood,' he says, 'very cohesive, very harmonious.'

When Hanif was fourteen, in 1979, the family moved to Walthamstow in London. Hanif never returned to school and now went to work with his elder brother first at a shoe factory in Hackney and later as a minicab driver, at which point the third and youngest brother joined them. 'From then on,' says Hanif, 'anything that we did, we did together, so all three of us continued to travel as one in life.' First they set up a workshop sewing the uppers of ladies' shoes, next a market stall, then a small factory making jeans and finally a car salvage business.

By the end of the 1990s the Qadir brothers were running a large garage and MOT centre in Walthamstow and they prided themselves on doing good works within the Muslim community there. They became weighty neighbourhood figures 'known for our unity', says Hanif, 'and because we went the extra distance to help others in difficult situations, sometimes by creating an element of fear. But we really did help people who couldn't help themselves.'

Hanif had always been the firecracker of the three. He says so himself. He was the one who had crossed a London street in 1979 to punch a boy who had flung a racist jibe – the first Hanif had ever heard – and in the years thereafter, he was the brother most likely to get into what he calls 'a scrap'. He shows a photo taken around that time of himself and his two brothers on a day out at a shooting range, all three grinning, guns in hand, Hanif with just the ghost of a black eye.

But suddenly the world – and their world – changed as 9/11 came and went. Hanif recollects thinking, as he says, 'Bloody hell, this is going to mess things up.'

It did.

'I felt like this is nothing to do with me,' he says, 'but I think people just started looking at us differently, or it was me thinking that, and because I had that perception, I started looking at people differently myself. It changed the way I was thinking.'

Hanif began to surf the internet for news about Afghanistan and Chechnya and he started to believe that this was not a war on terror but a war on Islam. He would sit up long into the evening discussing it with his brothers. These late-night debates and a certain chippiness about whether Mrs Smith had looked askance at his beard when she paid for her MOT today soon snowballed into something far more serious. How that change took place has everything to do with what Didier Long said about the influential power of people you meet at certain times in your life. And what is so alarming is that Hanif says the transition was 'very easy, just a series of incidents and circumstances that evolved until what manifested was a monster'.

In recent affluent years the Qadir brothers had been conspicuously charitable. People came to see them almost daily raising money for war- or famine-ravaged parts of the world. They would dish out a tenner here, fifteen there and feel like they were doing their bit for the global underdog. One day early in 2002 one of their regular customers brought along a man called Shahbaz, and here began what Hanif characterises as the long con. What would follow was all about building belief to trigger action, although Hanif seems to regard it today as little more than an old-style Coney Island trick.

Shahbaz, Hanif was told, was a brother from Afghanistan, '*talib talha*', a devout scholar who was raising funds for the orphans and widows of his homeland. His prosthetic leg only seemed to add to his credibility and he showed Hanif a little book he had brought along to explain how dire the situation was. 'Anything you can do to support us,' Shahbaz had said, 'even just pray for us.' Hanif handed over what cash he had and said that he would love to help more. That evening he got on the phone to his brothers and a few friends and the fundraising began. Soon many thousands of pounds had been raised, his wife had decided to sell her jewellery and there was even a degree of competition about who could raise the most.

Shahbaz came back over many days, soon bringing other pious men with him – an Algerian, a Syrian – and Hanif heard snatches of increasingly elaborate conspiracy theories about 9/11. 'We were sure these people wouldn't be lying. I mean, I'm not devout and these people are, so they must be telling the truth. I mean, looking back now, it was all a plan.' Hanif smoothes both hands down the legs of his jeans and looks down at a pair of incongruously shiny black shoes. At length, he says, Shahbaz disclosed that his brother was Taliban and the meetings now became more private, more urgent. They no longer convened at the garage but in Finsbury Park; mobile phones were handed over, their batteries taken out and locations often changed mid-rendezvous.

All this, bizarrely, sounded no alarm bells for Hanif. Instead he seems to have spiralled into some kind of delusion. It was exciting. It felt like this was real, meaningful work. And he remains adamant that violence was never mentioned, nor fundraising for violence. It was all about charity to the oppressed.

'It was a very subtle, very voluntary kind of approach, very clever, and they quote you chapter and verse about your role as a Muslim and then it's left to you to interpret. You are in that zone where you think that God's chosen you to do this. And I didn't get it, you know? I thought I'm not doing anything illegal. Absolutely 100 per cent naive, a real weakness.' Hanif shakes his head almost as though he is talking about someone else.

By the end of that summer of 2002 Hanif had convinced himself that only he could deliver the financial aid they had collected and undertake further good works in Afghanistan.

'I just wanted to get out there', he says and he shrugs. So the proposal was put to his Finsbury Park contacts and Hanif waited for their deliberation.

The account of the meeting which saw Hanif and a friend anointed for their journey to Afghanistan is surreal, to say the least. Shahbaz, who had just returned from the country where his brother had apparently been 'martyred by the Americans', broke the happy news. In the same breath he drew out a piece of fabric, 'like a handkerchief', says Hanif, a personal message of thanks from the Commander of the Faithful, written in ink and bearing some kind of official-looking seal.

'And I'm like, *Wow, thank God I'm worthy of this*,' says Hanif drily, 'and I said, "Can we see it?" I couldn't understand it because it was in Arabic, but sod everything else, I wanted to know where my name is, and there it was, so I said, "Can we have this?" The guy said, "You can take it, get it translated but then destroy it afterwards because it might get you into trouble." So we're sitting in the back of the car, me and my mate, on our way back from Finsbury Park and we're looking at it. He's got a tear in his eye and I've got a tear in my eye as well because we're these chosen guys. I felt blessed. We got back to Walthamstow at one o'clock in the morning to one of our friends who was studying Arabic, so he's reading it and he's going, "Fucking hell, this is really serious. This has got your name on it. It's from the top man in Afghanistan." And I went, "What, Osama Bin Laden?" And he went, "No, no, Mullah Omar", and he said, "You'd better get rid of this."' Hanif pauses and turns his watch on his wrist. 'It was almost a shame to burn it. I wanted to keep it as a souvenir, but we destroyed it. And then the next day I went to the travel agents and I said, "Book me a ticket. I want to go to Pakistan."'

Hanif wrote his will and within a week he was on the plane to Islamabad.

Hanif speaks of having 'become a very different person' within the space of six or seven months; it was a 'great change' of personality, he says. He became mistrustful of his own family, full of anger and hate, and he cites his vulnerability to such a transformation as lying within his tendency to over-emote, a naivety about his faith and (in an incongruous reminder of the violinist-turned-policeman Ed Coxon) a yearning for some meaning in life beyond simply making money at the garage. He also mentions more than once 'pretending you're something that you're not'. Although different in inception, this act of pretending can certainly lead to metamorphosis, as the sage words of Kurt Vonnegut recall: 'We are what we pretend to be, so we must be careful about what we pretend to be.'

Above all, there is also a curious passivity in Hanif's account, an abnegation of agency, despite having a character so clearly dynamic in many ways. He speaks of 'being pushed to a point where you think you don't belong', of being 'manipulated', 'exploited'. He asks, 'How could I get sucked into that?', couching his experiences in terms of 'what happened to me'. The cascade of his own poor decisions seems drowned, or at least diluted, in the recollection of how or why they were made, as he says, 'in a kind of trance'. It is almost as if the butterfly here is not the one that metamorphoses from wriggling caterpillar to beautiful airborne thing, but the butterfly of chaos theory, the one that flaps its frail wing in a far-off rainforest and unwittingly creates a tornado on the other side of the world. Perhaps a degree of denial is simply what you do when you have made choices in life that are well-nigh impossible to defend, as we have seen in the classic redemption narratives of offenders such as Ray Bishop.

In truth, much of the fevered contemporary soul-searching about radicalisation and deradicalisation hinges on a notional passivity that is simultaneously scary and neat. The idea that so-called brainwashing by the forces of evil can change people profoundly is uncomfortable, for sure. But it is less uncomfortable than acknowledging that previously kind sons and daughters, who studied for their exams and did the washing up when they were asked, then freely chose a course of action so abhorrent to the rest of their society. Hanif's story, with its darkly comic twists and turns – combined with his assertion that it never led to violent action – nevertheless offers a rather different, more nuanced picture. For the scope and reach of free will is a murky and much-debated commodity indeed. Perhaps a more pragmatic way of thinking about this sort of corruptive change, and also the journey back from it, is to focus not on the will alone but on how faulty our reasoning can become under certain sorts of pressure. And there is a lesson here for every one of us, not just those considering jihad or extricating themselves from it.

There are many different kinds of faulty thinking, but perhaps one of the most far-reaching and most interesting from the point of view of change stems from a phenomenon known as cognitive dissonance. Cognitive dissonance was unveiled to the world via one of the great psychological experiments of the twentieth century, undertaken at Stanford University, California, in 1959 by the social psychologist Leon Festinger.

The experiment itself involved getting some students to undertake a very dull task of turning some wooden pegs in a box for an hour. They were then offered differing amounts of money to lie to a third party about how interesting the task really was. A survey at the end showed that those who lied for a dollar were more likely to start believing their lie than those who lied for twenty dollars. They were more likely to start believing that this crazily boring task was actually quite fascinating, particularly when they were told that others had found it so. It was easier to change their minds, especially with the nudge of a group dynamic, than to acknowledge that as an honest person you were prepared to lie for a really petty, one-dollar reason.

The study had set out to prove under experimental conditions a hypothesis Leon Festinger first published a few years earlier. Festinger's interest lay in how we move to resolve the extreme psychological discomfort we experience when we hold two contradictory beliefs, ideas or values at the same time, or when we believe one thing and do another. Hitherto, his colleagues in this field had focused on behaviour and conditioning, but Festinger's point was that we do not just do – *we also think* – and that although we may not always be rational, we always rationalise.

His conclusion was that the discomfort of cognitive dissonance is so profound that our thought processes simply strive to resolve or reduce it as quickly as possible. That process of reduction can take various forms, many of them involving cooked-up justifications of one sort or another. Moreover, we tend toward what Festinger calls a 'drive state', blocking information that contradicts our beliefs and seeking out only that which confirms them.

The paradigm can be applied to a host of justifications right across the human spectrum from why I still smoke (even though I care about my health) to why I am cheating on my wife (even though I consider myself an honest, loving person), from why I claim I never really wanted the job in the first place (even though I spent months preparing my application) to why I am engaging with a potentially violent jihadi movement (even though I am a peace-loving Muslim).

Think for a moment about your own life and you will no

doubt be able to identify moments when you have resolved cognitive dissonance with a little wonky thinking of your own. And this may be the reason Leon Festinger's theory gained such extraordinary traction over the years; it is a cognitive mechanism equally willing to serve a gamut of beliefs and actions, either paltry or serious: the lure of a doughnut when you are on a diet or travelling to Afghanistan to work and even fight with the Taliban.

Festinger and the multitude who have pursued the many ramifications of cognitive dissonance have been chiefly concerned with how the pursuit of consonance causes us to delude ourselves. Yet in truth cognitive dissonance (and our response to it) thrums away in the background of many kinds of change, both negative and positive; it is one of the reasons we refuse to change our minds even when we should, but also why sometimes we do.

Not long after his arrival in Pakistan in 2002, Hanif Qadir would experience his own jangling blast of cognitive dissonance and one that he moved to resolve on this occasion not with faulty justifications but with a wholesale change of heart.

Hanif arrived in Islamabad on 5 December. He travelled across the city to a particular park, as he had been instructed, and called a number he had been given. He was told to sit tight. The following day he rang again, as instructed, and he was summoned to a rendezvous at a mosque in Peshawar. Hanif had asked how he would recognise the men he was to meet and he was told they would find him, ask him some questions and that here were the answers he should give. He duly travelled to Peshawar, made the rendezvous – 'They looked a bit dodgy to tell the truth' – and from there they took a taxi to a small town in the Khyber region, a few kilometres from the Khyber Pass. There in a dusty street in Landi Kotal, the taxi was swapped for a pick-up and on they drove.

Hanif did not realise that they had crossed into Afghanistan until one of the drivers said that they had just passed Torkham. This area north of the border was known to be the location of several Al-Qaeda training camps and Hanif was bound for a camp at Chelgazi – that much he knew – an hour or so north-west. But before they arrived, the pick-up stopped at a checkpoint where another car was waiting, and it was at this moment that Hanif's life would change direction. It was now that intuition and agency sparked to shape the next chapter in his life.

The men from the two vehicles got out and talked. A young boy of eleven or twelve also emerged from the other car and came over to Hanif's open window. He was bleeding and upset, words tumbling from him in broken Urdu. Hanif asked what was wrong and understood snatches of the garbled reply: 'Where are you going? If you're going there with them, these people are hostile. I'm from' – and the boy mentioned a village across the border in Pakistan – 'We came to help our Muslim brothers and they treat us like animals, like dogs. Don't go with them. These are not good people. They're butchers.'

Hanif got out of the car ostensibly to stretch his legs and asked the men what was going on with this boy. One of them 'almost casually', Hanif says, was hitting the boy's shoulder with the butt of his gun, and the old Qadir temper flared.

'I said, "What did you do that for? He's only a kid. Leave him alone." And the guy's ignoring me and says, "Come on, get in the car." I said, "No, what the hell's going on here? Is he telling the truth?" Because they were not taking me seriously or the kid and now someone's grabbed the kid and started kicking him and I'm going "Oi! Oi! What the fuck?"' Hanif is upright on his chair, really reliving this. 'And I pushed the guy away from the kid and then even the guy I'm with starts shouting at me and banging his gun on the ground. I started swearing in Punjabi, so we had a bit of a face-off. I mean he's only a little kid. He's wearing flip-flops, for crying out loud, and it was cold. OK, you're in a hostile environment, but you don't expect that from the people you're helping. So I just said, "Fuck off, I'm not going with you."'

Hanif waved some money at the driver of the other vehicle and, insisting that only he and the boy got in, they drove back to Landi Kotal. From there they took a bus on to Peshawar, where Hanif cleaned up the boy, gave him some food and rupees and put him on a bus back to his village.

Now in something of a limbo and convinced he must be with the wrong people, Hanif tried to call his contacts in Pakistan. No answer. He rang his brothers in London and asked them to reach Shahbaz and the others there. Again no answer. Confused and outraged, Hanif took a taxi to Islamabad – still no answer to his calls – and within twelve hours he was on a plane back to London. He drove straight from the airport to Finsbury Park, but there was no sign of anyone who had been any part of this. They had vanished like ghosts, and despite many days of calls and sitting in his car outside various mosques, he never saw or heard from any of them ever again. Hanif's days with the network were over.

'I do reflect back on that kid', Hanif says, now quiet again. 'He saved my life. I think it was divine intervention. I started to question all of that ten months of running around. All that passion. All that convincing my friends that it's the right cause. It was anger and anger and anger and anger and anger.' Hanif pounds a big fist on his knee. 'I'd left my wife and kids. I'd been prepared even to get killed, even to fight if need be. What would I have ended up doing? It was instant, a switch that went off in my mind. So in a period of a year I'd been through two different journeys, one the journey into this personality that I'm clearly not, the other this realisation that the path I'm being led down is not what it seems and I'm not that thick that I can't see through it. So in the end I really woke up.'

Hanif says that he thinks every single day about that experience and what a close call it was. He reckons it is inevitable that he would have come to his senses in the end, but if that had happened at the camp, how much harder and more dangerous it would have been to walk away. This, of course, all happened long before 7/7 or the notion of home-grown terrorism, so as 2003 got under way, Hanif now just slipped back into ordinary life in London with no visit from the security services, no explanations to give to anyone but his family. But he says that normality was never really restored after that. The experience of change and the journey back had left him a very different man, with a very different idea of brotherhood.

In 2003 Hanif and his brothers set up a gym and community youth centre on Lea Bridge Road in Walthamstow. This became the seedbed of an organisation they put together over the years that followed, called the Active Change Foundation. At first, it aimed to offer the neighbourhood youth alternatives to the evils of drugs and gangs. They ran workshops, sports events, outward-bound projects. Through this work they became aware of a rising tide of extremism among the Muslim youth of Walthamstow. Hanif began to find himself performing extempore interventions with young men and women he felt were at risk of going the way he had gone and he and his brothers put their concerns to the local council. But no one took much notice; not, that is, until the 7/7 attacks of 2005.

Thereafter the Active Change Foundation began to

receive funding from the British Home Office. The follow-ing year the infamous liquid bomb plot was uncovered. This was a plan by an Al-Qaeda cell based just down the road from Hanif's youth centre in Walthamstow to bring down seven transatlantic airliners with liquid peroxide bombs. And now Hanif found himself the unlikely figurehead of a deradicalisation drive that has rolled on – to much contro-versy and suspicion within his own community – ever since.

'The thing is that I was sold a lie,' he says, sounding calmer and more grave than he has for the last few hours, as if his new role in the world fits better than any before, 'and I see the same happening day in and day out to other young men and women. It angers me how those recruiters can create a walking, talking guided bomb, but what's the driving force behind the work I do today is exactly what happened to me, knowing what I could've done, where I could've ended up. Preventing somebody from falling down the same path just makes me feel a bit better. And we have. I strongly believe that somebody can change and I'd like to think that I know what I'm talking about. It makes me feel maybe I've saved somebody else's life and that lets me have some rest. It helps me overcome my own ghosts. It's made me who I am today.'

Some weeks later Hanif is a breakfast-time interviewee on BBC Radio 4's *Today* programme. He is talking about the unmasking of the IS executioner Jihadi John as Moham-med Emwazi in March 2015, and as you listen, you cannot help thinking it is a long way from painting Easter eggs with Mrs Braithwaite or stitching shoes in a factory in Hackney or indeed travelling to Afghanistan with the Taliban. This is change, real change, and it suggests that cognitive disso-nance need not always end in a spiral of delusion.

13

BEING WELL

The thought of painted Easter eggs can for some weak-minded souls hatch the thought of chocolate Easter eggs. And from there an anarchy of sorts is loosed. The seasonal confection propagates nightmarishly in the mind. Soon the desk must be abandoned in search of a little something. Would you excuse me for a moment?

But speaking of cravings leads us to an important point: that change is not always about what we believe, as for Didier Long, nor about what we do, as for Ed Coxon, nor even about who we are, as for Alina Simone. Sometimes it is simply about what we want, what we fancy. In this case, a Twix.

For many of us, the change that we would make if only we could get round to it is relatively modest. We would just like to take more exercise or stop smoking, lose a stone or two, and we cannot work out why it is often so incredibly difficult to do so. One might assume that big transformations require more effort and more resources than smaller changes. Learning to resist that mid-afternoon urge to eat chocolate must be easier than becoming a monk. But this is not necessarily borne out by our experience. Our trivial appetites and impulses seem to rage with a strange zealotry within us. While the four o'clock Twix may incur a twinge of regret, the very smallness of these failings seems often to afford them a kind of immunity to change. As we have learned, cognitive dissonance of this kind is very easily resolved with a skewed justification or two about why that particular chocolate bar, that cigarette at a party, that failure to go to the gym, did not count.

Yet, of course, years of smoking, physical inactivity and a bad diet are not small things at all. At worst they are killers and at the very best they are the primary lifestyle risk factors for an extraordinary gamut of ill health. Here would seem to be a reason, more compelling than most, to make a change. That is true both at the individual level and population-wide. The challenge – and the burden – of working out how to make such a change, both incrementally person-to-person and also at societal level, can hardly be overestimated. Tethered though it is to the most momentary desires, our well-being depends upon it.

Tall, lean and rather precise, Dr Paul Aveyard minds about this stuff. In fact, the Oxford University Professor of Behavioural Medicine and part-time GP minds so much that his life's work has chiefly been given over to finding ways of encouraging the public at large to alter their behaviour in apparently modest but life-saving ways. An authority on both smoking cessation and obesity management, his mission, like Hanif Qadir's, is to help people change. Unlike Hanif, Aveyard's focus is not the individual cases but how behavioural change might be brought to bear on a large swathe of society.

Also quite unlike Hanif, the professor's motivation does not lie in the fact that he has been there himself and come back from the brink. Indeed among the very first things he mentions is that people are always asking him whether he once smoked a lot, as if this must have led to his particular vocation. 'But I have never smoked', he says a little brusquely. 'Being a swatty kid, I never really came across situations where cigarettes were on offer, so it just never crossed my mind to smoke.' Paul is making coffee in an office kitchenette at the Nuffield Department of Primary Care Health Sciences and somewhat half-heartedly, he now offers a biscuit without taking the lid off the tin. 'I don't have one every day', he says and it seems proper to decline. Carrying the two mugs back to his office, their small columns of steam swaying in the sharp sunshine that streams in from outside, he proceeds to elaborate on what it was that put this fire in his belly about helping people to change.

'I know it sounds corny, but I think I always had that sense that I wanted to help people', he says, now perching very upright at his desk. 'I started my working life as a houseman, as we called them in those days, and I kept admitting the same people to hospital again and again and again. Patch them up, send them out and back they'd come. A lot of heavy drinkers, smoking-related disease, many of them from poorer backgrounds. So my key thought was that we ought to be doing better than this. Each person is helped, but we're not doing very much in the longer term for these folk.'

And so began a notable career in public health and the application of a public health agenda within primary medical care. The best part of a decade followed in smoking cessation research, from the efficacy of pharmacological treatment to reducing the uptake of smoking among school-children. And throughout, the driving question for Paul

Aveyard was not one of why or whether, but *how* effective change takes place.

Arguably the best-known 'how' model of health behaviour change is one drawn up in the 1970s by an American psychologist at the Cancer Prevention Research Center at the University of Rhode Island. James Prochaska's Transtheoretical Model, or The Stages of Change as it is more commonly known, was initially hailed as revolutionary. Chiefly geared to smoking cessation but claimed to be transferable to many change processes, the model can be thought of as like a little one-man play in five acts.

Act One is Pre-Contemplation, the stage in which our hero has little intention of changing his habits, certainly not in the next six months. Act Two begins when Contemplation kicks in, with an intention to change within the next six months. Preparation then follows as Act Three. This is when the intention is clothed in some practical ideas about how and when to do it (typically within the next month). The big drama then comes in Act Four, Action, when there is finally a change to get your teeth into; our hero stops smoking, eating too much or whatever the undesirable behaviour is. Big cheer, but no flowers on the stage yet, please. Because Act Five is Maintenance, the fifth and final stage, when the change still needs some attention and effort, but without the edge-of-your-seat jeopardy of the previous act. You may not be imagining queues up Broadway right now, but there we have it.

These Stages of Change are accompanied, according to Prochaska's model, by ten – yes, just ten – Processes of Change. Think of these as the actor's notes, from increasing awareness to self-reappraisal, from stimulus control to rewards that reinforce the change. And for those pesky changees who quit their bad habit but then relapse, there is the handy get-out of doubling back to earlier stages and beginning again.

Sounds neat – in fact, a bit too neat (not unlike those orderly stages of religious conversion). In some quarters there was certainly a collective sigh of relief, almost audible, that at long last here was a blueprint for how behavioural change takes place. The thousands of further experiments and interventions based on the Transtheoretical Model are evidence of that. But in other quarters there were murmurs, and even shouts, of dissent.

One such critique came from the mighty Albert Bandura – as you will recall, the father of Self-Efficacy Theory – whose ideas had been co-opted for part of the model. Bandura did not quite yell 'Poppycock!' but he might as well have done. In a terse broadside in the *American Journal of Health Promotion* he wrote that 'stage theories lead one into a thicket of problems. Human functioning is simply too multifaceted and multidetermined to be categorised into a few discrete stages.' He went on to assert that Prochaska's were not even real stages, but 'arbitrary ... contrived pseudo-stages' where the transition between one and the other might occur simply with the passage of time. Finally the business of returning to earlier stages when the transformation founders, according to Bandura, simply 'violates' the whole point of identifying stages in the first place. 'A butterfly has to be a caterpillar first', he fulminated. 'A butterfly cannot revert to a caterpillar.' His point was that stages only work as a way of thinking about this behaviour if they work. If they do not, then they simply end up getting in the way of change, rather than promoting it. You can almost hear Jim Prochaska say 'ouch'.

Around the time that Bandura's tirade was published in the USA, Paul Aveyard was working on a prominent medical trial in the UK of computerised interventions for smokers based on the Transtheoretical Model. When the results came back, Prochaska may have had cause to say 'ouch' once again.

'Our evidence was quite simple', says Paul. 'This doesn't work. People don't think in those terms of six months and one month, unless there's a very specific trigger, like "It's New Year's Day. I'm going to stop." They don't tend to operationalise their lives like that. So all this turns out to be very unreliable.' He straightens the keyboard on his desk. 'The theory just has nothing that's very accurate in its propositions.'

The professor shrugs, as though working on something for over three years that then turns out to be dead in the water is all in a day's work for someone like him; as indeed it is for all scientists worth their salt. Yet his enthusiasm for the work is undiminished. He still clearly believes in change, however frequently it may fail to conform to neat modelling, however mysterious its alchemy of the pragmatic and the intuitive.

'In principle I think we all can change. If you talk to people who've smoked, when they look back at their experiences they say, "Well, I tried it all those other times but somehow my head just wasn't in the right place and then it was", and they wouldn't necessarily be able to articulate why. I suppose my sense is that' – Paul pauses and spins the dregs of his coffee in their mug as if they might yield the answer – 'it just worked out one way or another. A coalition of factors came together. They got lucky. They either had better plans or they'd learned something or the external environment was more supportive on this occasion. And trying it lots of times gives them the best chance of success.'

Which brings us back to the thought of chocolate eggs and that vexed question of adjusting our appetites, of changing what we fancy. In 2009 Paul Aveyard strayed, half by accident, from the crowded research arena of smoking cessation into what he calls the 'very empty field' of tackling the rising epidemic of obesity. While the dangers of smoking were common knowledge by now, here was a new bogeyman. In 1980, 7 per cent of the adult population of the UK were obese. In 2003 that figure stood at 22 per cent, in 2015 at 25 per cent and its prevalence is projected to double over the next fifty years. Whereas there was now a half-decent system in place to help people stop smoking, even if there were still improvements to be made, Paul realised that for obesity there was 'absolutely nothing' he says, 'that looked like a system at all'. So he made it his new mission to change that.

Taking what he had learned about smoking cessation, the good doctor now began to apply that approach to how people might change their behaviour around food. He paints a picture of modern life as a kind of dystopia of indulgence (dressed up as freedom and prosperity) that prompts us at every turn to treat ourselves to something naughty but nice. And for many, that has spiralled into a relationship with food that is compulsive by any measure. Aveyard takes a pretty hard line on this. He feels that the strictures applied to tobacco advertising, taxation and most recently packaging should be extended to the foods that are turning his homeland into the fat man of Europe. However, he stops short of the oft-touted line that junk food is addictive.

'It's not, in any meaningful sense', he says, 'What you can say is that you show people pictures of different types of food and their reward centres light up with foods that we see as rewarding.'

'Chocolate éclairs.' This was an involuntary utterance.

'Yeah, well, personally it wouldn't light up for me with a

chocolate éclair,' says Paul, dead-pan, 'I'm not keen on those, but foods that are typically high in fat and sugar are what people seem to find rewarding.'

Perhaps most fascinating of all is that, while there is a statistic commonly bandied around that 95 per cent of obese people want to lose weight, many of them, according to Paul, do not want it *enough*. This is one of the big problems. They are not unhappy *enough* about it. These are not the 33-stone people, like Mike Waudby before his transformation. These are the averagely 'chubby' men and women with a body mass index of 30 or so. They would not call themselves obese, nor would you look at them twice in the supermarket, says Paul. And yet it is within this constituency that you find the large majority of the people at risk of diabetes, cancer, heart disease. If you want to change a population, as Paul does, then how you go about it is by changing these middling folk, not into super-slim gym bunnies, but into people who are a few kilos lighter on their feet, who have taken just one or two modest steps away from the destructive cycle of obesity.

Enter Professor Aveyard's latest large-scale medical trial. This is a study that goes by the name of BWeL and it captures the essence of what Paul Aveyard is all about. The core idea is that there is already a well-established nationwide proto-col of small-scale GP interventions that encourage people to stop smoking. At any given time around a million people are going through this system and it works, not wholesale, but pretty well. But there is no protocol for weight reduction and that is what the BWeL trial looks to change. This, it is hoped, may offer a pragmatic 'how' to the challenge of tack-ling obesity population-wide and with the tools at hand.

This is not an easy task. GPs often feel coy about bring-ing the subject of weight loss up for fear of giving offence and when they do, the standard litany of health warnings does not make much impact. People generally already know that they ought to lose weight, but that is very different from actively wanting or intending to do so. The belief is often there, but not yet the desire trigger for action. You can almost hear the jangling chorus of cognitive dissonance and the swell like some great national choir of justifications and avoidance that harmonises it.

So BWeL is exploring another approach altogether. It is based on a theory of motivation called PRIME, which connects behaviours such as excessive eating or smoking to momentary stimulus-induced desires, not unlike the chocolate egg moment earlier on. According to Paul Aveyard's hypothesis, the principle can be deployed to ignite a more dynamic agency-driven desire for change.

Over a period of three years and with participation from just under 2,000 people across sixty GPs' surgeries, the BWeL study is built to test the weight-loss efficacy of a thirty-second, scripted GP intervention that removes the 'ought to' altogether, while an experimental control retains it, focusing on health warnings alone.

Health cautions are replaced with a more open-ended approach by the GP, one that deploys not advice but assistance, not stipulation but that great driver of change, as we have already seen, the imagination. The patient is seeded with an idea of what doing something about his or her weight might look and feel like, a brief glimpse of a possible future. They are told that the best way to lose weight is to go along to Slimming World or Weight Watchers. Commercial group programmes like these were proved to be the most effective intervention out of six tested in an earlier trial by Aveyard and his team. 'I can refer you now for free on the NHS, if you'd like?' the doctor will say, turning to the computer to make the booking. 'Would you be willing to give that a try?' If the GP can secure that early agreement, he or she then says, 'That's great. But look, I know losing weight is hard, so come back and see me in a month', thereby creating subtle but strong threads of accountability and expeditious action, those other great drivers of change.

It sounds simple and not unlike an old-school sales pitch, but it is potentially revolutionary, as Aveyard says, 'just tipping the balance towards action as opposed to inaction. I mean we all want to change this, that or the other, so it's a sense of what does "want" mean in this context? So this is about creating desire at a gut level without having a long and complicated chat about why one should or shouldn't want to lose weight.'

What happens next, according to Paul, has nothing to do with willpower. Indeed, willpower is an 'unhelpful' notion that clearly irritates the professor, with its implication of a natural order of haves and have-nots. There is not much utility here for the concept of self-efficacy either; 'it has no population impact,' he says, briskly, 'because we just don't have the resource for lengthy counselling across the nation.'

Instead, Paul Aveyard's vision is all about the practicable, about speed and ease, the real-world currency of how to change on this scale. The mechanisms have much in common with many of the change stories in this book, but as though viewed from a great distance. It is a strategy that looks to lever open the door to a learning process in which large numbers of people make little plans (*I'm going to Slimming World on Tuesday*) which then lead to little rules (*I said I was going to walk not drive to the shops and I'm the sort of person who sees things through*) and in turn to little habits no longer requiring a strenuous effort of will (*I always go cycling on Wednesdays, I eat vegetables at every meal*). It is about not simply discussing but *enacting* modest, everyday, attainable change, but on a prodigious scale.

'I guess this is the theme of what I do,' Paul says, glancing out of the window to the street below, 'that the most important thing is to provide as many opportunities for people to change as possible, just simple prompts, but it's that prompting that I think is key. We've all got motives to do this stuff inside us. There are people out there who are at that point right now' – he taps the desk – 'that you could just tip by giving them the right thing at the right time. I think that is probably the most important thing we can possibly do.'

And quite suddenly, for all the talk of just tipping or a-kilo-here-a-kilo-there, you can see that this is not a modest change at all, but a potential throng of small metamorphoses, a seething cloud of many millions of butterflies. Perhaps it is the grandeur and, yes, the beauty of this aspiration to Be Well that accounts for why Professor Aveyard is so very understated, so matter-of-fact, so clearly cautious in his optimism. The work will not be done in his lifetime. There is no epiphany, no Damascus Road moment on the way, but it would be hard to find a more hopeful change project. Or indeed a more generous one.

14

WHITE BEARS

Being well is, as it goes, one of the key pillars of contentment. Or so a silver-haired Carl Jung, smouldering pipe in hand, told a journalist from the *Sunday Times* just a few weeks before his eighty-fifth birthday. Asked what he considered 'basic factors making for happiness in the human mind', the Swiss psychiatrist and father of analytical psychology offered a list of five. He touched on beauty and friendship, work and religion, but number one was 'good physical and mental health'. Music to Paul Aveyard's ears, no doubt.

The interview with Dr Jung in 1960 came as he was finishing work on the manuscript of an autobiography that would be published two years later, after his death. Within a chapter entitled 'Late Thoughts', the old man reflected not on the secret of happiness but on morality and what he regarded as the two great evils of the twentieth century. The first 'outpouring', he wrote, had been in Hitler's Germany, the second in Soviet Russia. His point was that simply seeking out the opposite of evil – 'Good' – and then 'succumbing' to that instead was no way to dispel the terrible shadow that had been cast. It was the *succumbing* that was the problem. 'Every form of addiction is bad,' he wrote, 'no matter whether the narcotic be alcohol or morphine or idealism.'

A bitter epitaph for the century, perhaps, but what does it have to do with change? Well, sometimes change does not relate to our physical appetites or behaviours. It is not about work or religion or love. It is not even about our vices or our personal obstacles – or certainly not at first glance. It is about ideals, what we believe about the way the world should be. As for Emily Lau in Hong Kong, it is about politics.

Numerous psychological and sociological studies over several decades have demonstrated that in fact our baseline political orientation is among the more stable of our attitudes. While our views on specific policies or individuals are as flexible as any other, the broad inclination of our political outlook tends to be formed early in life and then sticks with us for the duration. As changes go, a substantial shift in political orientation is a rare beast indeed – and we are not talking about policy U-turns here or politicians who party-switch for expedient or gestural reasons. No, we are talking about a deep change of *ideology*. We are talking about people like Salomea Genin and how her political world-view underwent a revolution of its own.

It is so unseasonably hot in Berlin for mid-April that one cannot help feeling one's own convictions of every stripe – political, ethical, personal – all melt one by one into a soup of indifference to everything but a nice, cold drink. Suddenly one of those fruit, syrup and ice concoctions with a silly name, on sale at a certain prominent coffee-house, sounds a siren call. This is just one of any number of flagship

outlets of global brands that teem beneath a criss-cross
of tram wires around Hackescher Markt, in the centre of
what used to be East Berlin. The dated-futuristic Berlin TV
Tower, that icon of the GDR, still pops its globular head
above the brand signage. But it is a very different world and
a different life here from what it was a little over fifty years
ago, when Salomea Genin's nine-year application for GDR
citizenship was finally accepted. Yes, you have not misread it;
while East Berliners in their droves were fighting to get out
of the GDR, Salomea was fighting to get in.

She lives today a short walk from Hackescher Markt,
down a narrow side-street with treacherously uneven paving.
The door opens to a narrow slice of an apartment with very
tall windows, open to the sweltering late-afternoon heat.
With a bustle of chatter, Salomea leads the way inside,
saying rather loudly that she has mislaid her hearing aids
and patting a table covered with a blue and gold embroidered cloth in search of them.

'I lost my gold-framed glasses on here once for a whole
day', she says. 'No matter. I'll be alright. Now, let's put all
your contact details in here first.' And she scurries over to a
gleaming iMac, its box still on the floor by the desk.

'I've just got it. It's very intuitive.'

Typing fast with two index fingers, the meeting is duly
logged. She clearly likes to keep a note of such things. Then
Salomea rummages urgently among a pile of papers, with an
energy that belies her eighty-two years.

'I want to read you something', she says, and with no
further explanation of why or what it is, she pulls out a piece
of paper, straightens her glasses and, standing by the desk,
begins there and then to read in a strong, clear voice:

> Then, perhaps, life only offers the choice of remembering
> the garden or forgetting it. Either, or: it takes strength to

remember, it takes another kind of strength to forget, it takes a hero to do both. People who remember court madness through pain, the pain of the perpetually recurring death of their innocence; people who forget court another kind of madness, the madness of the denial of pain and the hatred of innocence; and the world is mostly divided between madmen who remember and madmen who forget. Heroes are rare.

Now Salomea fetches a carafe of water and two glasses, and it is only when asked that she says, 'It's James Baldwin.' Then she sits down to tell her own story of remembering and forgetting.

Salomea was born into a Jewish family – 'a dysfunctional one', she says – in Berlin in the summer of 1932. The youngest of three sisters, she was just four when her parents separated. She saw her father once again when she was six 'and then', she says 'he disappeared out of my life'.

Now, nearly eight decades on, Salomea summons a series of terrifying tableaux from her early childhood under the Nazis. Her memory for detail, complete with nuggets of dialogue, is astonishing, a talent that would be turned to a different use later in her life. She describes, when she was four or five, being pulled into the shelter of a doorway by her sister as the Brownshirts marched through their Jewish neighbourhood singing a song with the line 'When Jewish blood spurts from the knife, then everything is good'. 'I mean, I understood that,' she says, 'and of course my sister was scared and this fear passed itself on to me.' Or there was the time her mother sent her with her blonde hair and blue eyes out for a pound of mincemeat on the Day of National

Solidarity, three weeks after Kristallnacht in 1938, when Jews were not allowed on the streets; a boy she knew spotted her and barked at her, 'What the hell are you doing here? Off you go home! If I see you here again, I'll report you to the Kreisleitung of the Party!'

In May 1939, not long before the little girl's seventh birthday, her mother secured passage to Australia and Salomea escaped from Berlin.

Her political awakening came five years later, in Melbourne, when she was just twelve. Her elder sister had joined the Communist Party and one day in 1944 took her along to the Eureka Youth League, the young Communist organisation in the country.

'And there', she says, 'I heard the General Secretary of the EYL telling us about socialism. She starts talking about Germany and that the persecution of Jews had come about because they needed to divert from the social problems they were having. When I heard that, the world suddenly' – Salomea makes a gesture with both hands as of a little firework exploding – 'there was suddenly an explanation for the things I'd experienced and why we'd had to leave. There was clarity. And I was hooked.'

Salomea was soon one of the Eureka Youth League's brightest and most committed young activists. For her it became, she says, 'a substitute family'. However, when the Second World War ended and the Cold War began, Communists, even young ones, became public enemy number one. Their meetings were denied venues, their activities disrupted.

'It caused us to close in on ourselves', says Salomea, glancing out of the window as the setting sun pulls a bank of shadow up the steeply pitched red tiles of the church roof opposite. 'And the stronger the pressure became, the more people like myself, really committed Communists, were convinced that the socialist countries are the goodies and the country I'm living in, they are the baddies. All the stories that were by then being published about the gulags, they were lies, slanders of socialism. We just didn't believe them.'

At just seventeen Salomea joined the Communist Party itself and the following year, in 1951, the World Federation of Democratic Youth organised a World Youth Festival, to be held in East Berlin. Salomea leaped at the opportunity to return, much to the bewilderment of her sisters, who swore they would never set foot on German soil again.

'Wait a minute', says Salomea, now rising from her seat and going next door to her bedroom. There is the sound of drawers and cupboards being opened and she emerges a minute or two later with a large silk scarf, a commemorative souvenir of the festival. Printed on it is a circle of young people of all nationalities, holding hands around a globe, above which a vast dove hovers. Dressed in bright, hopeful colours, they are all smiling and beneath each pair of hands clasped in friendship is the word 'peace' in assorted languages. At the edge, written in red, modern sans-serif: 'Youth unite in the fight for peace against the danger of a new war!'

'So yes, it was strange to go back to Berlin,' says Salomea, carefully folding the scarf again, 'I mean, I had my memories, but on the other hand it was fantastic, because I knew – I'm now saying this sarcastically – I knew I was going to my anti-fascist state and here on the ruins of that horrible system, they – or we – were building a new and just world. I wanted to stay for six months, but the bloody bastards, as we say in Australia' – Salomea laughs out loud at how Australian she sounds – 'didn't let me. And the bigger the hurdles to staying, the more I was convinced this was where I belonged.'

Salomea Genin says several times in the course of what

turns out to be a long, long conversation that, for her, socialism again and again trumped human relationships. The
cause and the Party were simply more important than any
member of her family, any lover, any friend. They became
what Salomea today dubs 'false gods'. And in 1954 she left
her mother and sisters in Australia and moved back to West
Berlin with the express intention of securing her passage to
the East. Her conscious reason was profoundly ideological.
'I wanted to build the new world', she says. But she spec-
ulates this evening as to whether there was not also some
kind of unconscious desire to be accepted by the so-called
Aryans who had persecuted her family and her people. 'Like
a Stockholm Syndrome,' she says, 'I think that feeling along
with the suppressed fears of my childhood in fact dominated a lot of my actions throughout my life.'

There is a silence and she gets up to creak the tall window
shut against the cooling evening outside. Now she begins
to describe her nine-year-long efforts to gain citizenship of
the GDR. She could cross the border back and forth on her
Australian passport, even after the Wall went up, but the
GDR authorities would not grant her leave to move there.

Then one day, three months after the Wall went up in
1961, Salomea was approached in the street by a stranger.
He explained he was a friend of a friend and asked if she
might like to join him for coffee. She did and it was pleasant
enough, so he asked to meet her again a week later. This time
he brought along another man, who introduced himself as
Comrade Pohl, from the Ministry of State Security. Pohl
said that now the anti-fascist protective wall had gone up,
they needed to know what was going on in the West and
would Salomea help them.

'This was one year off my thirtieth birthday', she says, 'I
was lonely. I missed the political activities from Melbourne,
that feeling of belonging, and I thought, well, this will be

my contribution to the class struggle. I had no ambivalence whatsoever. I said, "Yes, all right, I will".

Salomea Genin became an Inoffizieller Metarbeiter or IM (informal collaborator), an informant for the Stasi. At their request she immediately stopped moving in progressive circles, broke with current friends and adopted an outwardly anti-GDR stance. They would ask her to take coffee or a walk in the park with certain people, sound them out on particular issues and report back fortnightly. After eighteen months of this, Salomea's nerves were in tatters, the isolation psychologically untenable. She crossed the border and called Comrade Pohl, requesting a meeting. When he arrived, she said that she could stand it no longer and that, if they would not let her come and live there in the East, where she could find a husband and make friends, then she would leave Germany for ever and forget about the GDR.

'And he looks at me' – Salomea lowers her glasses for effect – 'fatherly, mildly, friendly, and he says, "Well then, *Wir werden dich hereinbringen müssen*. I suppose we'll have to take you in, won't we?"'

Salomea took up residence in a tiny flat in Treptow in East Berlin on 16 May 1963 and began work as a translator. In the mid-'60s she had two children with a man called Hans, but the relationship did not last long and she raised them alone. Meanwhile, her IM duties continued, as they would for nearly two decades. Accounts were gathered of whoever she had met – friends, lovers, colleagues, passing acquaintances – what they had said, their moods and plans, all of which Salomea would commit to her extraordinary memory and then repeat to Pohl and a succession of other Stasi handlers, who would write in their notebooks or occasionally record a detail or two on a Dictaphone.

For twelve years, she says, she had 'no qualms whatsoever, because protecting the cause of socialism and the GDR was

the important thing in life. I didn't feel it to be any duplic-
ity', and Salomea holds a gaze so unwavering as to make this
rather extraordinary statement entirely credible. It is almost
dark outside now, but she seems oblivious to the fact that
she is sitting in a grey half-light. Only when prompted does
she say, 'of course, of course' and get up to turn on a tall,
plain standard lamp.

According to Albert Camus, the real prophet of the nineteenth century was not Karl Marx anyway. It was Fyodor
Dostoevsky and it is from a political travel essay that Dostoevsky published in 1863, *Winter Notes on Summer Impressions*, that the inspiration for a famous psychological experiment comes – one that sheds light on Salomea Genin's story
and her imminent change. Dostoevsky wrote:

> Try to pose for yourself this task: not to think of a polar
> bear, and you will see that the cursed thing will come to
> mind every minute.

In the mid-1980s, this line captured the imagination of
an American social psychologist called Daniel Wegner and
he set about testing it under laboratory conditions.

Wegner asked a group of volunteers to vocalise their
stream of consciousness for five minutes and to try hard not
to think about a white bear, but to ring a bell if they did.
Sure enough, the white bear won through; the bell chimed
on average once a minute for each participant. The same
group was then invited to think of white bears as much as
they could for another five minutes. At this point the group
thought of white bears markedly more often than a different control group who had been invited in both exercises to

think of the snowy carnivore as much as they liked for the allotted 300 seconds. Wegner was moved to conclude that attempted thought suppression has a paradoxical effect as a self-control strategy, only redoubling the force with which the undesired thought will 'rebound' later.

The experiment spawned a whole new field of psychological research dubbed 'ironic processes theory'. It has been fine-tuned over and over, with other thoughts less suited to a Christmas card and potentially more troublesome for the heads in which they are lodged. Wegner's conclusion was that when we try to suppress a thought, one part of the mind does so quite effectively, but that another 'checks in' to make sure the thought is not cropping up, thereby ironically returning it to centre-stage. As Wegner and others showed in a host of related experiments, there are strategies that we can use to keep those ursine thoughts at bay: distraction, postponement to an allotted time later in the day, avoiding overloading the mind with multi-tasking, meditation, even intense exposure to the thought.

But this much is certain: simply decide to forget an unwelcome thought, be it mid-afternoon chocolate, a broken heart, or the realisation that your utopian dream of a better society is a sham, and you are on a hiding to nothing. You will remember and remember and remember.

We have seen how unwelcome thoughts and information spark processes that can change the way we think profoundly. Salomea Genin's story is certainly alive with the whispering rationalisations that follow cognitive dissonance. But the ideological metamorphosis that was coming for Salomea may owe more of its 'how' to the ironic processes of Dr Wegner and his legion of white bears.

Perhaps it was inevitable that the centre could not hold. Or perhaps it was a series of accidents that it did not. All that Salomea knows is that over a period of about seven years from the mid-1970s through to 1982, everything changed – or she did. But from an ideological conviction staunch even to the point of betraying every human relationship she had, it would be a long road back.

It started with a few troubling inconsistencies between what she had understood socialism to be when she had learned about it in Australia and what she found here in the GDR: comrades who were autocratic, uninterested in any political debate. These 'white bears' did not change Salomea's ideology, but they did make her think that perhaps she had got some of the theory wrong. She applied to do a part-time philosophy course and began to learn how ideologies become established and also how they become corrupted.

'And by the time I'd finished it I knew two things', she says. 'One was that my lack of education in Australia had caused me to think in terms of black and white; and, two, that I was no longer a Marxist. That was rather a shock. Of course, I didn't say it out loud, but I knew from then on.'

She mentions jokingly the letter by Marx in which he had written 'If anything is certain then it is that I myself am not a Marxist', but there is no levity when she describes a mur-mured coffee-break discussion in 1975 among a few of her fellow students about censorship in the GDR. She had later asked a friend who had been there about it. This woman had turned to her and said – Salomea repeats it in direct speech – '"They're so schizophrenic they don't even realise that what they say in private is the opposite to what they're saying in public." And that sentence, it went like a bolt of lightning into my guts' – Salomea punches herself quite hard in the solar plexus – 'because she had just formulated something that I had begun to feel but didn't want to believe.'

Suppressing the full implications of that lightning bolt, that unwanted shift in belief, to the farthest corner of her mind, Salomea nevertheless began to self-censor what she told her Stasi handler. And like trying not to think of a white bear, again and again she found doubts about the GDR surfacing in her thoughts, like a chorus of so many reasons to change her position. There was no separation of state powers, no freedom of assembly or of the press, no freedom of speech or of movement. These moments of realising, as she says, 'that the Emperor was naked' were powerful, but she continued to push them away.

'Because I still didn't want to know it,' she says and shaking her head she says it again, 'I still didn't want to know it. I'd been completely incapable of facing up to the fact that this socialism is not working, because it would have done what it then did when I faced up to it: made me sui-cidal. Because for thirty-eight years' – Salomea drums the table with one fist – 'I'd been a highly convinced, dedicated, devoted Communist.'

Finally one day – with typical precision she names it, 2 September 1982 – the doubts could be suppressed no longer. Salomea experienced a second and this time devas-tating unravelling of her belief system, a blow so powerful that it would prove a catalyst for active change. She was standing in front of the television waiting for the Western news to begin and the announcer mentioned a forthcoming series of films about National Socialism, building up to the fiftieth anniversary of Hitler's rise to power.

'I heard this,' she says, 'and a question that had always bothered me and I'd never been able to answer came up in my mind. How come that the Germans had claimed not to know what was happening to their Jewish neighbours? Where did this schizophrenia come from? And suddenly the sentence that six years previously had gone into my guts like a bolt of lightning, the two schizophrenias, they joined, and in that second another thought came up and it took my breath away. You are living in a dictatorship, a banal police state as they have existed throughout the ages, and what's more, you have helped to make it so. And that was when I fell into a deep black hole and I knew I couldn't work with the Stasi any more.'

Remember Didier Long and that idea that you do not believe what you do, but rather *do what you believe*? Well, now those seven years of shifting belief brought forth the essential component of all change: action. When Werner, Salomea's Stasi officer, next came to see her, she unleashed a tirade about the GDR administration and a few weeks later she mustered the courage to break contact altogether. As it turns out, Werner protected Salomea. In his report of the meeting, delayed for two months, he wrote nothing of what she had said, but that she appeared psychologically frail and was of little further use to the Ministry. 'The contact will be gradually faded out', he concluded. And that was the end.

For Salomea there followed three years of deep depression and two more of therapy. But finally, as the Wall came down in 1989, she began to work out that the only way to make this change real and to survive the feelings of guilt that had come with it was by somehow sustaining the action that had seen her break with the Stasi. And in Salomea's case that meant talking; it meant remembering, not forgetting.

First she confessed face to face to a college lecturer whom she had reported on in the 1960s. Then she began to write about her Stasi involvement, give interviews. It was an unorthodox move – most of the 170,000 or more IM informants just melted back into society – but for Salomea, bearing witness worked. This was the 'how' of her change, an antidote to all those years of suppressing certain thoughts. And it still works today, not removing the guilt but making it possible to live with.

'If I hadn't talked about it so openly,' she says, 'nobody here would know anything about me working for the Stasi. Most people don't do this. But I feel I need to forgive myself.'

'And have you, Salomea?'

'More or less. By the time I was about seventy-eight' and she laughs. 'What has really changed for me is the attitude that there is a cause which is more important than anything else in life. I don't have such a cause any more. In that respect, I'm a fundamentally different human being to what I was forty years ago. You know, I love sayings and the one I really like is, *Dear Lord, give me the serenity not to want to change what I can't, the courage to change what I can and the wisdom to tell the difference.* Another is *Fighting for peace is like fucking for chastity.* I find that very funny and very true.'

As the church bell chimes ten o'clock in the dark street outside, she goes off to find a ball of rainbow-coloured wool to show. She calls from the room next door that she is planning to knit a blanket from it. 'It's all plain stitch', she says, and, as she natters away, you get a feeling that somehow Salomea Genin wants neither the interview nor the bearing of witness that has powered her change to be over.

15

ON HAPPINESS

That business of remembering, however central to Salomea Genin's change, is nevertheless a very different kettle of fish from *experiencing*. And this difference turns out to be of material importance for those of us intent upon tracking down the holy grail of so much desire for change: happiness. Remember Colin Price saying, 'Of course there is nothing more to life than happiness'? Well, the issue gets knottier when we try to work out what exactly happiness is. That is a question that has everything to do with how and what we remember.

The psychologist and brahmin of our cognitive illusions Daniel Kahneman points out that 'the remembering self' is quite distinct from the psychological present of 'the experiencing self'. The remembering self has little regard for those moment-to-moment sensations or perceptions as David Hume cast them in his 'bundle theory'. Yet it is the remembering self, according to Kahneman, that is the curator of our past life stories and the arbiter of our decisions about the future. It is the remembering self which first imagines

– and then reckons that it knows – what will make us happy or unhappy. And of course, in a classic Kahneman twist, it does not always get this right.

One of the fallacies to which this leads is what Kahneman dubs the focusing illusion. This is when we give undue emphasis to a single aspect of something that is, in reality, multilayered. This illusion is particularly prevalent when we consider the possibility of a future change in any significant part of our lives. What we do, according to Kahneman, is underestimate how good we are at adapting and therefore overestimate the impact any such change would have.

The study in which Kahneman, along with the psychologist David Schkade, proposed this focusing illusion took as its starting-point the fame of a particular psychological paper published in the 1970s. To widespread astonishment, this paper had suggested only modest differences in life satisfaction between paraplegics, lottery winners and people who had neither hit the jackpot nor lost the use of their legs. The fact that these findings are so counter-intuitive as to be newsworthy – indeed they were exaggerated in much of the coverage – Schkade and Kahneman took to be a prime example of the focusing illusion. We are surprised, they argued, because we overestimate the extent to which a lottery windfall would make us happy as Larry and paraplegia the very reverse. When we imagine such turns of fortune, we focus on the moment of change, the *becoming* paraplegic or stratospherically rich, and mistake it for the experience of *being* paraplegic or stratospherically rich, which is altogether different.

The Schkade and Kahneman paper went on to demonstrate the focusing illusion further through an experiment showing that people expected life satisfaction to be higher in sunny California than in the windy, cold Midwest, whereas in fact it was pretty much the same. They called the paper

'Does Living in California Make People Happier?' and concluded with 'a moral and a warning: *Nothing that you focus on will make as much difference as you think.*'

Dr H'Sien Hayward lives in California and she is, as she says with a swish of a long, silky ponytail, happy. Warm, brimming with smiles and animation, she seems it. She also studies happiness, so you get the strong impression that, one way or the other, Dr Hayward knows what she is talking about.

For her doctoral thesis in psychology at Harvard University, published in 2013, H'Sien Hayward decided to replicate the famous well-being study quoted at the outset by Schkade and Kahneman. She argued that the original study's findings had often been misrepresented, even by Schkade and Kahneman, and that the paraplegic subjects were in fact shown to be markedly *unhappier* than their experimental controls in the original 1970s figures. The literature of adaptation and rehabilitation had done little to resolve the ambivalence. It was full of conflicting evidence, one side citing evidence of the lasting negative impact of adversity, the other dead-set on this so-called hedonic treadmill model, suggesting that no matter what good or ill fortune befalls them, people return to a stable level of happiness after time.

H'Sien Hayward set out to iron out some of the flaws both in the original trial and in its confused legacy. She duly assembled another cohort of lottery winners, people with acquired spinal cord injuries and regular experimental controls. However, this time she made one key difference: she lengthened the time since the big win or the big accident from a year, as in the old study, to more than a decade. And her findings turned out to be startling. Like the first study, the lottery winners seemed to have got used to their electric gates and swimming-pools, but among those with the spinal cord injuries there was a substantial difference from the initial findings. By every established metric of happiness available they were just as happy as the lottery winners and the experimental controls. What had not quite worked in terms of adaptation at one year after the accident, at ten or more years now resoundingly had.

'And I was shocked,' says H'Sien, her brown eyes wide, 'I twisted it and I controlled for different things. I sliced and diced the data, but there was just no difference on any measure of happiness.' She beams a perfect Californian sunburst of a smile. 'So that was very exciting, but then the differences that *did* exist were even more so, because I don't think everybody had the *same type* of happiness. It is the nature of the happiness that seemed to change. So with a lot of money, happiness might have more to do with pleasurable activities because you can afford them, but it might not be infused with a lot of meaning. Whereas with people in wheelchairs, maybe their level of pleasure isn't quite as high, because they spend half their day trying to navigate the world, but they are more likely to find what they are doing in life meaningful. And meaning is a huge component of happiness.' Metamorphosis indeed.

This gravitation following adversity towards a different kind of happiness is part of a psychological phenomenon called 'post-traumatic growth', explored in numerous studies since the 1990s. We can all probably think of one or two people for whom a bad experience – illness, trauma or bereavement – has fostered a new sense of purpose in life, closer relationships, a reordering of emotional priorities. Well, that is post-traumatic growth and it nuances Schkade and Kahneman's conclusion that '*Nothing that you focus on will make as much difference as you think*'. The point is that an experience of life's fragility and its cruelty does not always produce either pathological effects or none. It also sometimes produces positive effects. Indeed, they come about not in spite of adversity, but because of it. Think of Shander Herian. Think of Hyppolite Ntigurirwa.

Pondering the *how* of this particular vein of change, H'Sien Hayward's own research went on to show, in a second longitudinal study over eight years, that the happiness scores among her spinal cord injury subjects seemed to go hand in hand with a new bias of memory towards recalling positive over negative stimuli. In short, there grew a tendency of their 'remembering self' to see the sunshine, not the cloud.

'And yet,' says H'Sien, 'happiness is not the story society tells about disability. So I'd wanted to do something tackling this stigma but using a scientific method. Because I think that these things that would typically be called tragedies are also transformative experiences. They just rip apart your priorities and there are so many ways to respond when life does that. One of them is to break, but another is' – she searches for the words – 'to grow. And I guess I have this fundamental belief in the power of change in the darkest of circumstances. I think for all people at all times there is hope, which is not to minimise anybody's personal suffering. I just think there is always that ability to change your state.'

You may be wondering at such powerful conviction from a young scientist with many of her research years still ahead of her, but in a way H'Sien has been researching this subject for most of her life. Because there is something else you need to know about Dr Hayward. She is paraplegic. And that is not the only grave adversity she has had to face in her life.

H'Sien Hayward grew up in a woodland homestead in the tiny community of Lopez Island, off the coast of Washington State. Her parents were hippies and here in a house they had built themselves, H'Sien and her brother, Rishi, older by eighteen months, were raised in idyllic barefoot freedom. Brother and sister were inseparably close, but one day there was a terrible accident. Rishi was on a tractor with his father in the woods, the tractor tipped and the ten-year-old was crushed and killed.

'I do have a flash-bulb memory from that time', says H'Sien. 'Sitting on the couch and my mom's friend walking towards me after getting off the phone to her. Mom and dad were at the hospital. I could tell from her face that my life was going to change for ever and everything just slowed down. And I felt that if I could just slow it down a little bit more, it wouldn't happen.' She pauses. 'He was an amazing little soul, the centre of my life at that time.'

From the awful days that followed, H'Sien identifies two key revelations that in some way set the tone for the life that followed. One was her mother's remarkable attitude to what had happened, that they should not be grieving or focusing on the loss as much as feeling gratitude that they had known Rishi for a whole decade. 'And that really, really changed me', says H'Sien. 'It prepared me in a way for what happened to me seven years later.' The other revelation was the nine-year-old H'Sien's discovery of her own personal panacea for trauma, one that she would have cause to deploy more than once in her life.

'My second most striking memory is standing by myself outside the house' – she makes what looks like a little shudder, one tress of brown-blond hair falling to her cheek – 'and all of a sudden being struck by the most piercing inner anxiety that I now had to do everything because my brother had been the athletic and social one and I'd just been the academic one. It was like, *How am I going to do it all, how am I going to do everything?* So this is the other thing that really changed but also probably got me through it. I just' – she smiles and shrugs – 'got busy. It was a complete identity transformation.'

From mousy and bookish, H'Sien now signed up for all the school sport teams. She got a boyfriend, 'Yes, at nine,' she laughs, 'and I've never been single since'. She became the life and soul of her social group. She would make lists of what she had to achieve: state volleyball champion, straight As in all subjects, dating the quarterback, running seven miles before school every day, being prom queen. One by one she listed her goals in her journal and one by one she ticked them off.

'This was the way I conceptualised being perfect at that time and that if I went fast enough maybe nothing bad would catch up with me. Because my brother's death didn't make any sense. That was what I was trying to keep ahead of, like trying to hold it all together, but with scotch tape, so that if I dropped it, my life' – she cups her hands, as though holding something delicate and precious – 'it would break, but as long as I just kept holding it and moving fast and putting that tape on it, then everything was going to be OK, because' – she takes a breath – 'well, I knew that it could so quickly and so easily not be.'

H'Sien now flips back from bereaved child to psychologist mode, an apparently effortless transition that she makes to and fro a number of times in the course of the morning. The profoundly personal and the searchingly theoretical seem to sit comfortably together in H'Sien, like two old friends who agree and sometimes disagree but are content in one another's company, natural together. And the reason for this may lie within the theory she has just begun to describe with scholarly animation.

This is an account of the cognitive mechanism behind changes in identity and behaviour in the wake of trauma. The idea comes from the work of Ronnie Janoff-Bulman, one of the psychologists who pioneered the study of post-traumatic growth and a co-author of the original study of lottery winners and paraplegics. Janoff-Bulman's theory is that of so-called Shattered Assumptions. This describes how trauma splinters the 'assumptive world', our implicit and widely held view that the world is benevolent, that things happen for a reason and that, if you are a good person, then the things that happen are also generally good. When that world-view is fractured by personal disaster, then a new one must be rebuilt from the shattered pieces, with new beliefs and new purpose. This, according to Janoff-Bulman's theory, is one of the key mechanisms by which many people change profoundly in the wake of trauma. And this is important, for it would happen to H'Sien: it is change rather than some mollifying sense of healing that allows life to begin again.

Seven years after her brother's death, H'Sien was in Hawaii on a sports scholarship to a boarding school on the Big Island. She and a few of her friends were on their way to the beach to celebrate their victory in the state cross-country running meet earlier in the week when their car crashed on a winding road. H'Sien was thrown from the vehicle. She broke her neck and her back and spent the next ten days in a coma. She has no memory of the accident and only what she calls 'little tinny memories' of her early days in hospital, but as the weeks wore on and the pain meds wore off, the reality of what had happened to her began to bite. Her broken neck had been stabilised, but her back was broken at the fourth thoracic vertebra, mid-chest.

'I remember feeling down from my neck to my sternum and noticing how it changed, how it felt normal up here'

– H'Sien touches the soft hollow between her collarbones with a fingertip – 'and then when I got to my sternum, it didn't. I remember feeling this sharp pain of anger and it wasn't at the driver. It was at the doctor because I felt, if they weren't going to fix me, then why didn't they just let me die, because I felt like perfection was no longer attainable. That's what I thought the goal of human life was after my brother's death and I felt like I couldn't be perfect now because I was broken.'

This was the shattering of 'the assumptive world' and two weeks of blackest depression followed. Just as after Rishi had died, she had gone to sleep each night praying that she would wake up in the morning and he would be alive, now she went to sleep praying that she would wake up and be able to walk. But then H'Sien Hayward did what H'Sien Hayward does in the face of disaster.

'I got busy again. I started making lists.' She writes an imaginary one on her hand. 'So Tuesday would be learn-to-put-on-my-socks-by-myself day. On Wednesday I would learn to bath myself. And the busier I got, the happier I got.'

So it was that this old adaptation took on a new form. A new world-view began to crystallise. In lieu of snaring cute boyfriends and winning state track meets, there were now 'virtues', as she calls them – 'Tackle Anger' was one – scattered in among the pragmatic nuts and bolts of learning to live with a disability and plans for her academic career. Again her mother's optimism that she was alive and that life was going to be wonderful, in her words, 'undergirded' these years, as well as a sense that they would have given anything for Rishi to have been paralysed rather than dead. That was what she calls the foundation for her new life.

For about five years, learning to walk again remained high on her list. The year after the accident she spent four months in a clinic in Southern California learning to walk with leg braces and electrical stimulation. Although it technically worked, it was not particularly functional. The apparatus was cumbersome and time-consuming and over the years that followed, that initially overwhelming priority of walking receded. It dropped down the list and another assumption morphed. What was 'transformational' about this spell in Southern California turned out not to be the walking at all. It was the crowd of cool, good-looking young people with interesting lives and real hopes for the future who, like her, had no use of their legs.

There are many ingredients that H'Sien cites as having helped her over the years that followed to form a new world-view and a new life for herself, the 'how' of change for her: a period modelling in New York (she is a beauty) and a good deal of intrepid foreign travel, wonderful friends and a supportive family, deep meditation and, perhaps above all, her academic vocation as a psychologist. All these allowed her not to break but to bend and grow, just as the theory of shattered assumptions and post-traumatic growth suggests.

Yet H'Sien is at pains to point out that there have been many very difficult times too. These are not when she falls out of her wheelchair. 'It happened twice yesterday', she says, rolling her eyes and laughing. 'Doesn't bother me. It's humbling, like a reminder that there's a bigger picture.' She says the really tough times are when she is congratulated upon seeming happy 'even though you're like that'. She suddenly fiddles with the strap of her sun-vest and looks hurt. 'This happens so often, usually strangers. So what I'm saying is that I am OK except when people tell me that I'm not, that my life isn't worth living in their eyes.'

And this leads H'Sien to a powerfully redemptive assertion, one that runs counter to so many commonly held ideas about people in her position.

'Because,' she says, clearly aware that this is not the

expected script, 'in some ways my disability was the best thing that ever happened to me. It changed my life so fundamentally. And sure, it's hard sometimes, but I definitely think I am wiser and have a greater capacity to live with my eyes open and remember what's really important. I think part of that does come naturally with age, but when profound change is thrust upon you, it's like being offered an elevator instead of having to walk up the stairs to get to some of these places.'

It is during a discussion of what happiness is and whether any experience is so dark as to preclude the kind of redemptive change H'Sien Hayward has been talking about that she mentions her favourite book. It is, she says, *Man's Search for Meaning* (1946), by the Austrian psychiatrist and concentration camp survivor Viktor Frankl. Here Frankl identified a will to meaning as the primary motivational force within human beings, writing of how he saw it played out even in the midst of the most atrocious suffering in Auschwitz. It is in meaning, according to Frankl, that the key to happiness lies.

'It is characteristic of the American culture', he wrote in a postscript to the book from the 1984 edition, 'that, again and again, one is commanded and ordered to "be happy." But happiness cannot be pursued; it must ensue. One must have a reason to "be happy." Once the reason is found, however, one becomes happy automatically.' And according to Frankl, such a reason can be found even when it seems to be most elusive. 'Even the helpless victim of a hopeless situation,' he concluded, 'facing a fate he cannot change, may rise above himself, may grow beyond himself and by so doing change himself.'

This idea of happiness as more than simply pleasure is an ancient one. The Greek philosopher Aristotle also put happiness – and, by implication, change in its pursuit – at the core of his ethical thinking. His watchword was *eudaimonia*, one of those slippery and much-debated philosophical terms that invests happiness with an ethos that is about more than beer and skittles. Contemporary scholars tend to translate *eudaimonia* as 'flourishing', but the point is that it is not a passive state. It is an activity full of human agency and focused on the habitual practise of the virtues that make up the Good Life. It is not something you are; it is something that you do. As Aristotle put it in the *Nicomachean Ethics*, 'this activity must occupy a complete lifetime; for as it is not one swallow or one fine day that makes a spring, so it is not one day or a short time that makes a man blessed and happy.'

And H'Sien agrees, throwing back her head in laughter, 'Oh yeah, I'm totally in the *eudaimonia* camp.'

H'Sien Hayward is now taking what she has learned both in the ivory tower and in her own life struggles out into what can often be a cruel world. Academia, however gilded the institution or legendary the teachers, did not on its own quite answer what she calls the 'so what?' question. In an echo of Ed Coxon's story, a robust answer to the 'so what?' has become a big part of meaning and happiness for H'Sien. She is currently in psychotherapy training and anticipates a career divided between academia, where she says she hopes to add to the knowledge base of 'what it is and takes to be happy', and clinical practice, where 'people can touch and feel and live it'. She has recently worked with genocide survivors in Rwanda and Tsunami victims in Thailand and she is now working with Vietnam veterans with post-traumatic stress disorder in California.

H'Sien visibly lights up when she talks about this work – and you can see why. Because here so much of what we have learned about how to change seems to coalesce. She speaks of the power of stories like hers to open up new sets of options, new beliefs and even to be an imaginative catalyst for change among people struggling with traumas of their own. That is the mysterious, intuitive and sometimes revelatory part of how we change, the light-bulb moment that we have met in this book time and again, from Didier Long to Salomea Genin. H'Sien also talks about the sustained hard work, the learnable skills and new habits that can be brought to bear in the change process. And this, as we have seen, is all about pragmatic, deliberate agency, the *doing* rather than being. This is the other part of how we change or help others to do so, whether it be Mike Waudby on his cross trainer, or Paul Aveyard scripting his weight loss interventions. It is in its way a fine example of eudaimonic activity. Aristotle would surely approve.

As her parting shot, before she wheels her beautiful way off to class, H'Sien Hayward says something that reverberates for a long while after: 'Not everybody wants to change, but I think that getting a sense that life is fragile and has an ending can really light a fire under you. It's a call to action. For me it was the realisation that if I simply let life happen to me, I wasn't necessarily going to like what happened and I realised that wasn't enough for me, that I also wanted to play a hand in creating my life and that there is a timeline' – she grabs a sweater and a book from the desk and puts them in her lap – 'so I'd better get moving.'

PART IV

CHANGED?

16

I AM THIS

I live in a wooded valley carved deep by a river that is always changing, never still. Or almost never. It did stop dead one winter a few years back, at the end of a long cold snap. A flowing, shifting mosaic of great chunks of ice that had formed upstream locked one afternoon and sat there immobile for three or four hours, as though to give the lie to Heraclitus. Reason dictated that the water continued to flow beneath, but it was a curious illusion, as though the natural forces of time and change had been paused by some mighty unseen finger on the remote control. People stopped their cars on the bridge to look. They got out, leaned over the balustrade, took photos. Someone said that old Albert remembered the river doing this once when he was a child, but that must be getting on for eighty years ago now. I found myself thinking that it would be fun to try and walk across, but this was an irresponsible idea and I am a grown-up, so I did not articulate it, although I do still wonder sometimes whether it would have been possible.

That same winter I had watched my father, now at the

very end of his life, lying on a bed, his head tilted to one side to look out through the metal bars of a safety rail at the sunlight coming in through the open door of his room. Only that morning I had seen the youngest of his five grandchildren do the very same thing but through the wooden bars of a cot, watching motes of dust glitter and swirl in the first sunshine of the day. I had wondered whether some fragmentary memory of being an infant in a cot remained within this very old man I loved. But more than that, I was struck most powerfully by a thought so obvious I was surprised it had never occurred to me before: how all that separated and connected those two different states of infancy and old age was in fact nothing more than a succession of days, a day after a day after a day after a day. The baby and the old man he becomes eight decades later, whatever changes befall him, whatever changes he makes, are the same person. It is some metamorphosis indeed and some extraordinary continuity. I did not articulate this idea either.

I mention myself at this point in a book that is not about me because the whole idea of identity is somehow easier to think about within the intimacy of 'I', 'me' and the people I know and love. Please try it yourself: find a photograph of yourself as a child and attempt to recall what that child thought and felt, who he or she was. I have one here. I am with my mother this time. She is around the age that I am now. She is wearing a loudly checked smock with the distinctive lank collars of the 1970s and my two year-old-self is leaning against one of her legs, in a little green flowery dress and a pair of long white socks, one of which has fallen down. I have no recollection of when or where this picture was taken, nor in truth much of what it felt like to be that little girl. There are glimpses, but I have no way of knowing whether I have made them up. In the facts, that little girl is long gone, but I do recognise her as *my* past and no one else's, a kind of magnetic north from which I have gone on to live my life and experience my own changes, both organic and deliberate. I feel I owe her something, although what I am not quite sure.

This is the part of change that so many of those *Change Your Life in Seven Days!* self-help manuals and step-models miss out. Yet it is fundamental to the metamorphosis story. Change sits at the porous outer borders of who we are, fascinating and mysterious, because however transformed, no one ever actually becomes a different person. Change is only meaningful in terms of identity because in part *we also stay the same*. The caterpillar and the butterfly are the same single creature. And so it is that the stories of change in this book are only stories at all because they are also stories of continuity.

The eighteenth-century philosopher John Locke was another sober Enlightenment empiricist who, like David Hume, never married or had children. Locke was not roly-poly though; in fact, quite the reverse. Tall and lean, with sunken cheeks and soulful eyes that seem too large for his head, Locke had a cast of jaw that makes him look in every extant portrait as though he has just taken a mouthful of something not altogether as tasty as he was expecting.

It is perhaps this expression of vague discomfort that accounts for a version of the Ship of Theseus thought experiment known as John Locke's Socks. Although found nowhere in his published works and probably apocryphal, it offers a neat reminder of the paradox of change and continuity that faces any of us when we look back on our lives. It goes like this: John Locke has a hole in his sock and he has it darned. A thrifty fellow, when a second hole appears, he has that darned too. And a third, and a fourth, until the material of the old sock dwindles. And the question is this: at what point does the philosopher's heavily darned hose cease to be the same sock altogether? When does *changing* become *changed*?

In fact, academic philosophy has not much troubled itself with the process of how individual human beings change. Rather, it has looked to the very opposite: how we remain the same, what glues us together as people over time. And John Locke was no different, although a pioneer of modern thinking in this area. He resolved the sock/ship paradox as it relates to personal identity by distinguishing between what it is to be human in a physical sense and what it is to be a *person*, one who can 'consider itself as itself' with all the psychological hinterland that that entails.

To illustrate, Locke came up with another thought experiment, this time confirmedly his own. The soul of a prince, all his thoughts and his memories, is transferred to the body of a cobbler, whose own soul has departed. Far-fetched, I know, but stay with me. Although now in a different body, the prince, so argues Locke, still considers himself the prince and herein lies the essence of what it is to be the same person over time. It lies in his consciousness and his continuity of memory, not his body. Thus began a philosophical quarrel that rolled from Locke to Hume and on across the centuries to today, when philosophers still debate the primacy of body over mind or mind over body as the anchor of what makes a person a person even as they change.

'The trouble with Locke's idea is you can't separate pseudo-memories from real memories. You need an audit trail of some sort and it's the body that provides the audit trail.

Remembering oneself is such a gigantic task. You can only remember bits and sometimes they'll be flattering bits or they'll be the things that you did wrong. Whatever it is, it's always overlaid by stories you've told or been told.'

The philosopher, eminent physician and old-school polymath Raymond Tallis is sitting in a hotel bar in central Manchester with a large glass of pinot grigio in front of him and Bruno Mars piping rather loudly through the hotel sound system. Professor Tallis has asked, most courteously, if this background music might be turned down, but a hatchet-faced waitress has said, gesticulating to a deserted bar, that she has the other customers to consider. 'Never mind,' says Ray brightly to her already turned back, 'we'll manage. Thank you.' And he dives into a hotchpotch of memories of his own: his anarchic glee at knocking over a mud castle his brother had built for him when he was about five; his wonder at his first sight of the sea at St Ives a few years later; walking on a beach with his wife and then teenage sons some time in the 1980s and feeling very happy; the crushing regret when an infant who had been admitted to A&E in the 1970s died very suddenly on the ward; looking at some fishing nets as a teenager in the early 1960s and being engulfed by a wave of existential angst out of nowhere although this is hard to imagine now, as Ray cheerily dives from one fragment of recollection to another.

Tallis is one of Britain's most distinguished gerontologists, but alongside a thirty-six-year career in medicine he has also produced more than twenty works of philosophy, generally written in the hours between 5 a.m. and the start of the NHS working day. His philosophical calling came to him as a teenager, initially as a palliative to that bout of anxiety when he was fifteen. Later, as a doctor, philosophy continued to be a way of extending the idea of human beings as medical organisms that are born and die and investing it

with something more of the wonder, complexity and beauty
of the human experience in between. Philosophy has been
for him, he says, 'a sheer joy of trying to turn ordinary wake-
fulness into something that's astonishing'.

His thinking has emerged from many dozens of num-
bered notebooks going back to the mid-1960s. He shows
one, a black hardback volume that he takes out of his brief-
case. '*Pensées*, I call them,' he says and laughs his head off,
'and then there are the whinge diaries and I've got very,
very large numbers of those, but they have got more and
more focused. It's such a wonderful way of being outside of
oneself. Certainly philosophy is a habit. It's a retreat and it's
a vocation.'

Tallis has agreed to meet with the disclaimer that most
of his work on personal identity has, like other philosophers, focused on what stays the same, rather than what
changes. Change in his own life – and there has been 'lots'
he says – has not come through discrete life stages so much
as through the proliferation of simultaneous selves. Tallis
the doctor. Tallis the philosopher. Tallis the poet (he does
that too). Tallis the son. Tallis the husband. Tallis the father.

'You have lots of micro roles, so you become all of those
things and of course each one is utterly transforming. And
you internalise them, those performances. You are never one
role. There's never that luxury. You have a multiplicity of
roles, a family of selves. So yes, there's an awful lot of change,
but also an awful lot of continuity. I have a sense simultaneously of the self as just a colloidal suspension of fragments
but also of it as something very coherent.'

Ray Tallis has spent more than twenty years pondering
this continuity, this coherence, and getting scratchy with
each of the available philosophical theories. These range
from Locke to Hume to the wild sci-fi thought experiments of the mid-twentieth century – brains divided and

transplanted into different heads, entire bodies scanned, destroyed and the information beamed to outer space where the person is reconstituted, all thoughts intact – to the latter-day materialists' insistence that we are bodies and nothing more. Instead, Ray simply argues that we are the only entities in the universe who enjoy such a profound relationship to the past, present and future. He calls this 'temporal depth' or – with a chuckle – 'a fat now'. It is this 'fat now' that, according to Ray, feeds an intuition of identity, a feeling of Being Me, that does not resist change but simply absorbs it.

'That I Am This', says Ray suddenly, tapping his fingertips on the lapels of his tweed jacket before holding out both hands and looking at them. He pauses while the idea sinks in and Bruno sings about love in the background. 'If I've ever had a fundamental thought, it is the astonishment That I Am This. And, do you know, I can remember first feeling it. I was standing with my friend Chris, in our flat in Oxford when I was a student. It was in the attic we shared, very cheap, stank of cabbage soup, and suddenly I had an overwhelming sense That I Am This. *I Am This*. And I guess that's been the absolutely central thing that's driven all of my thoughts since. That is the lynchpin, the founding moment of personal identity, and it incorporates everything, both a very long series of memories and, you know, also the organism.' He tugs at a tuft of his beard just hard enough to pull the skin away from his jaw for a moment. 'And I mean, however changed you are, there's always been continuity, some kind of internal stitching. You have never broken off being yourself during the process of change.'

And the philosopher-physician grins, takes a large sip of his wine and watches smiling as the idea resounds like a bell with so many of the conversations that have gone before this afternoon: Didier Long and his 'one life', Ed Coxon and the tunes still played on his fingers, Alina Simone's 'same husband, same face', Shander Herian and his 'blind habits', Mike Waudby and 'the 33-stone guy that'll always be with me', Ray Bishop and 'the real Ray [that] shines through'. For anyone fearful that making a change may compromise their identity, that 'changed' will be an unfamiliar or even hostile land, a glass of wine with Raymond Tallis might very well be prescribed by way of assurance to go ahead, to make the change; you will still be you.

17

VIOLET K.

'Have it', Raymond Tallis had said, handing over a volume
of his poetry – 'I can't shift them, to be honest' – and he
had laughed and signed the frontispiece, 'Thank you for
the lovely conversation'. Indeed, researching a book like
this, one picks up all sorts of precious souvenirs along the
way. The yellow love-and-peace ribbon from Emily Lau.
An Alina Simone album on vinyl. A DVD of an orchestra
playing Schönberg, Ed Coxon among the violins. Even a
rare breed of snowdrop, now planted in the garden, from
a remarkable man we shall meet anon. But above all there
are dozens upon dozens of photographs of the people whose
stories have filled these pages taken at different times in their
changing and changed lives.

There is little Hyppolite Ntigurirwa three years after
the Rwandan genocide, standing with his brother at their
school, dressed in the same lichen-green he was wearing
that day at the university. There is Peter Holmes with his
twin and his sister laughing in the sunshine of their great
uncle's orchard the day before the jet-ski accident. There is

twenty-one-year-old H'Sien Hayward, sitting up on a bar in New York City, every inch the glamorous model and with no outer sign that this was the year she finally acknowledged she would never walk again. There are the lean features of the now round-faced Didier Long back in the black monastic habit of Frère Marc. There is the straight-faced black-and-white portrait of a three-year-old Shander Herian, brushed, pressed and standing with his now dead father's hand on his shoulder.

There is also a photograph, again in black-and-white, of Violet K. as a toddler. She is dressed in a perfect little white frock with Peter Pan collar, embroidered bodice and puffed sleeves, her podgy hands at her sides and expectant rapture on her face. She is standing in a handsomely proportioned sitting-room with large lamps and paintings in the background and she appears to be looking out of a window, as if all the world were waiting for her out there.

'My real first love – even now as I'm talking about it, I can feel it in my body and I can really remember – ' says Violet K., some forty years later, 'was freebasing cocaine.' She closes her eyes for a moment. 'And I can even remember where I was the first time. It was a Monday morning. We'd been up all night on MDMA and we're now in somebody's kitchen just off the Gloucester Road, and we smoked it on the foil. Actually it's much better in a pipe. You get a better hit, but this was in 1986, I was just a kid, you know? Fifteen or so. So I ran this clear fluid down the foil. I can remember breathing it in and it was just so pure, so easy. I thought *hahhhhh*' – Violet's breath aspirates loudly, intimately – '*this is incredible. I want to feel like this forever*. It's like you breathe in and you breathe in and you breathe in and your lungs fill up and fill up and you're taken over by something immensely powerful. I don't know how else to describe it. The closest I ever get to feeling it today – and it's a long way off – is when I'm swimming. If I do a lot of lengths, I get that feeling of my lungs expanding and I get a bit of a chemical high from the exercise. Yeah, it's like breathing in life force and power and a sense of invincibility.' Violet smiles and, with a little shiver, draws a pink pashmina around her shoulders. 'So when I smoked heroin I was really quite disappointed at its quality and how different it is. Heroin became my love, of course, but initially it was that freebase cocaine. It's just the most incredible feeling.'

A year later, when she was sixteen, Violet first tried heroin. She stole some from a girl with whom she was sharing a hotel room in Barcelona, where they had gone with a party crowd for a few days.

'I proceeded to then smoke her heroin with her but presenting it as my own', says Violet with cut-glass precision. 'The thing is I was just desperate to connect, desperate to have intimate relationships with people and I got that through using drugs and through sex, of course. A teenage girl with no boundaries, that's going to happen a lot', and she offers a tasteful sofa throw to put over the knees. 'It's cold, isn't it?'

At first, it is hard to tell whether Violet K. is consciously trying to shock. She says things like 'I was surrounded by people with money, but I hadn't got any of my own, unless I stole it from my stepfather's wallet when he was in the bath' or, a bit later, 'there was one guy who liked me to kick him very hard, wearing pointy stilettos and each time he'd give me a twenty-pound note, so no holding back there'. Listening to these disclosures so early in the morning only adds to their disquieting effect. The incongruity is further magnified by the fine Georgian room and the fact that these words spill from a well-spoken, educated woman who minds whether you are warm enough and how you take your tea. Yet over the hours that follow, it becomes clear that Violet has no intention of shocking for its own sake. It is rather that the combination of vivid awareness of her past excesses and the very act of disclosure, without filter or nicety, is part of the cure; it is part of what brought her back from all this. But not before she had spiralled into places that make free-basing in Kensington or chasing the dragon in Barcelona seem fairly salubrious.

Violet grew up in London, where her father ran a pub in the heart of Knightsbridge. In that phrase alone you catch a glimpse of the dual nature of Violet's childhood, half well-heeled, half shabby-decadent. On the one hand, there was the nanny, the best private schools, the gentility of the area; on the other, there was the pub downstairs from their flat, the drunk people asleep on the stairs in the morning, the strippers on Thursdays, the lock-ins, the poker games, the seedy side of life that would later have its draw for Violet.

'I mean, it's the soil, isn't it?' she says, shrugging. 'I'd internalised a lot that I'd grown up around, the drunken-ness, the sexualised environment, the looseness, the escape, the fantasy. I still love the smell of cigarette smoke now.'

When her parents' marriage failed and her mother left, Violet was just old enough to be growing conscious of class and difference at her smart private girls' school on Sloane Square. She says she grew ashamed of her background, sloppy and chaotic as it was. When her teenage rebellion came, some years later, it focused on this tension between never quite fitting in with her posh, wealthy friends and the lure of low-life glamour.

The turning-point came when Violet was twelve. With her elder brother she watched a video of the cult film *Christiane F*, based on the true story of a fourteen-year-old heroin addict and prostitute in 1970s Berlin.

'And I just thought it was the coolest thing I'd ever seen in my life', says Violet. 'Dangerous, sexy, dark and all with a David Bowie soundtrack, who I loved. So I just built a fantasy world from that. I didn't want to be all these things that I felt I should be or people were telling me to be. *Oh Violet you're so clever, you should be a doctor or a lawyer.* No, I'm thinking, *I'll be Christiane F, that's what I'll do. That's who I'll be.* Because I couldn't identify with these people around me.' Violet looks out of the window as the slow morning sun begins to warm the golden stonework outside. 'I was twelve then and more or less by the time I was twenty-two I was Christiane F. You know, Paddington Station, Sussex Gardens, King's Cross.' She smiles and counts London's red-light roll-call on her fingers. 'To the point where I actually felt I had embodied her. It sounds odd, I know, but I remember one time I was rifling through my mother's drawers looking for money to buy drugs and I remember thinking *Wow this is what she did. She did this.* And from there sinking down, down, down, down, down, down, down, into the real squalor and degradation of being a heroin addict. I wanted that from *Christiane F.* Sometimes I fought it, but once I realised I was in my own film, it was easy.'

W. H. Auden wrote in *The Age of Anxiety*, 'Human beings are, necessarily, actors who cannot become something before they have first pretended to be it.' You could call it a reaction to cognitive dissonance; certainly it turns out to be resonant both of Violet's decline into drug addiction and, nearly two decades later, of her journey back from it.

From watching *Christiane F* to freebasing with the decadent trust-fund kids in Kensington took two years. Violet skipped school after that. There were visits from truant officers, arguments with her mother, but none of it made much difference. Two years more and she was on heroin. A job in a hostess bar followed, where the stiletto-kicking story originates, then some waitressing at an upmarket pizza joint in Chelsea. There another waitress, also from a privileged background, 'taught me how to be a junkie', says Violet, 'a proper one': how to inject, how to manage dosage, cook up, keep the cash flowing by shoplifting clothes, making small faults in them, then returning them and pocketing the money. Perhaps it was inevitable that prostitution was the next thing on the learning curve and supplied the revenue stream that would follow. Certainly the *Christiane F* blueprint suggested so.

'We cross boundaries in life, don't we,' is how Violet puts it, 'in all sorts of ways, good and bad. And if you're in the throes of addiction, it's not that you don't care. You can't care. It's desperation. A withdrawing heroin addict will do almost anything not to feel like that and it always involves money. So by the end of my career as a prostitute' – Violet laughs out loud – 'A fantastic thing to say, isn't it? But by the end I could make a lot of money very, very quickly, but there was no glamour involved and it was a tenner and a tenner and a tenner and a tenner.'

One can try to hold a poker face during testimony like this, but Violet clearly spots something that moves her to offer a small consolation.

'Yes, it was revolting,' she says, leaning forward, 'I know, but I don't think I was ever out on the street for very long. As long as I'd got £100, that would last me until the next evening. And then, you see, heroin takes away any need for anything else. People on heroin are like kids. They're babies, all snuggled up in bed together, no sex, just eating Ready Brek, baby food, you know? And that's what I would go back to. So, yes, there is the dangerous side of being Christiane F, working the street, shoplifting, stealing handbags, but there was also this side that was just the baby thing. *Oh lovely get under the blanket.* It felt safe, cosy.' She looks down and smoothes the throw that is over her knees and then goes on without looking up, 'Although of course what you realise in the end is that it's an illusion and people will stab you in the back to get drugs, because I certainly did. So ultimately there's just unbelievable loneliness and a fear of never being part of anything ever again.' She looks up. 'Can we take a break?'

Violet rolls a cigarette and steps onto a narrow wrought-iron balcony to smoke it. Then she lights some incense and boils the kettle for more tea. She said early on that in nine days' time she will have been clean of drugs for seven years, but as she now bustles in her kitchen offering sundry herbal infusions, she does not look or seem like someone with two decades of full-blown smack addiction and prostitution behind her, not to mention a smattering of minor criminal convictions (although no prison). Yet this, says Violet squeezing the peppermint bag in her cup, is where outsiders always tend to get it wrong. There was no single trajectory up or down. She says this quite sternly. Change, certainly for Violet, did not come like that. The desire came early, the change itself late. Even being changed would be no arrival, but a lifelong activity.

From her early twenties Violet was in and out of rehab. 'In and out, in and out', she says. 'That story goes on and on, a year clean here, then not and then two years and then not.' Sometimes she was partying with hedonist aristocrats, sometimes she was not partying at all, sometimes she was turning tricks for a single heroin score on a King's Cross street, these different worlds shuffled like so many playing cards. Of the much-fabled 'rock bottom' so idiomatic to drug recovery, Violet says drily, 'Well I had a few.'

The final one came in October 2007, when she was thirty-six. Her latest relapse had hit her hard. This is the first time she mentions her then ten-year-old son Sebastian, who had been born during a clean period and who had lived with her on and off since. But that year Sebastian had moved permanently to live with his father and Violet had fallen apart. Within a few months she was living in a room at a homeless hostel in Earl's Court, drawing dole fortnightly, which she spent on one score of heroin, cornflakes – she would steal the milk, she says – and a weekly litre of methadone bought from an ex-boyfriend nearby. The bottle lived under her bed and she describes a cycle of knocking herself out with it, then coming to, drinking some more and lapsing back again, 'like living in a coma,' she says, 'the most miserable, solitary existence ever'. This was the grim fulcrum on which Violet's life finally began to turn. 'I just knew I had to do something. I knew the drugs had to go. That was it. That was when.'

It has been mentioned that the greatest philosophical minds have chiefly preferred to focus their brainpower on how we are, rather than how we change, but a notable exception comes in the neat personage of a French philosopher of the late nineteenth and early twentieth century, Henri Bergson. With tidy moustache, high starched collar and a pair of eyebrows so extraordinary that they look like they might have their own ideas, Professor Bergson arrived in Oxford in May 1911 to deliver two lectures at the University Examination Schools entitled 'The Perception of Change'.

'The point is,' he told the rapt crowd of his subject, 'that usually we look at change, but we do not see it. We speak of change, but we do not think about it. We say ... that change is the very law of things: yes, we say it and we repeat it; but those are only words and we reason and philosophise as though change did not exist.'

How Bergson then illustrated his central contention was not by deploying some fantastical thought experiment with ships and socks and cobblers, but simply by swiping his hand through the air from, so he said, position A to position B. The point he was making with this momentary gesture is one with which this book and the people in it have wrestled again and again. We tend to try and understand the movement by breaking it down into a series of static positions. We believe that when we understand those positions, we understand the change. Wrong! cried the Frenchman. It is the movement itself that is reality, the static positions merely imagined and indeed downright unhelpful if one is to apprehend the true nature of change.

'I have spoken of movement,' Bergson concluded, 'but I could say the same for any change whatsoever. All real change is an indivisible change. We like to treat it as a series of distinct states that form a line in time ... But nowhere is the substantiality of change so visible, so palpable as in ... the continuous melody of our inner life ... Our personality is precisely that.'

The idea of change as an indivisible reality, a continuum rather than a destination to be reached in timely fashion, might ring some bells in this damp church hall in a London suburb a little over a century after Bergson gave his famous lecture.

It is 7 p.m. and one of over 30,000 weekly meetings of Narcotics Anonymous across the world is just beginning. This is an open meeting, so it is larger than some. There are sixty or seventy people in the room, all sitting on metal framed chairs laid out in a semicircle and were it not for the long oilcloth banners hung from the rafters with the Twelve

Steps and the Twelve Traditions printed on them, you would not immediately identify this as a group of recovering drug addicts.

There is a young man who smells of aftershave, groomed and alert in sharp suit and shiny shoes. There is a pregnant woman with her eyes closed and both hands making little circles on her bump. There is an older man with concave features, perhaps a dearth of teeth, in a tracksuit that is zipped up right under his chin. There is a woman in her sixties, with a beret and blazer garnished with gold buttons that catch the fluorescent light above.

A heavy-set man in his fifties gets up and introduces himself. 'I'm J – and I'm an addict', and so begins a fifteen-minute oration that has all the hallmarks of the finest public speaking in the TED sincerity model. He talks about the fear, the loneliness, the 'fucking madness' of his addiction. He talks about the connection and the love that he has felt through the fellowship of these meetings, how they have helped him take it one day at a time. All around the room, people smile and murmur assent. He says how people both inside and outside NA often struggle with the idea of the 'Higher Power' that is writ large within the Twelve Steps, but for him that Higher Power had always been about the connection in the room. 'It's amazing here,' he says and takes a deep breath which he blows out as though it were smoke, 'yes, it's amazing here'. And something happens that is rare at Twelve Step meetings, certainly in the UK: the room erupts in cheers and clapping.

Then a middle-aged woman who is chairing the meeting gets up and, a little deadpan, goes through the 'anniversaries', as she puts it.

'Anyone here thirty years clean?' she asks. Two hands go up, and there is a ripple of applause.

'Twenty years clean?' Seven hands go up. More applause.

'Ten to fifteen?' she says. Another five hands and further clapping.

And so she continues until she gets down to 'Anyone here clean for thirty days?' Half a dozen hands go up and the biggest cheer of the night shakes the rafters, as the newly changing look about the room with vulnerable smiles. There follow some two-minute 'shares', as they are called, some more coherent than others, some with accounts of recent travails, some of long-past lows or highs. Each opens with 'I'm Xxxxx and I'm an addict', regardless of how many months or years they have been drug-free. Each closes with a spontaneous *sotto voce* of 'thank you's and 'well done's from the crowd. Then everyone rises, holds hands and together they say the closing words of every NA or AA meeting anywhere in the world, in the form of a prayer to 'whatever you take to be God'. They are the same words that Salomea Genin had quoted at the end of that long evening in Berlin: 'God give me the serenity to accept the things I can't change, the courage to change the things I can and the wisdom to know the difference.' And with that, everyone spills back out into the dark street and they go their separate ways.

What is so fascinating about the Twelve Step model originally devised for Alcoholics Anonymous in the 1930s (and now deployed by addicts various the world over) is that while 'working the steps' is a key part of the process, recovery itself is without end. Changed you may be on paper, clean of drugs or alcohol for decades, but still you stand up and say 'I'm an addict', in a haunting reprise of Ray Tallis's 'I am this'.

For outsiders this can prove a little confusing. It is as though a butterfly were to stand up at Larvae Anonymous and say, 'My name is Eric and I'm a caterpillar'. Well, apparently not. For like Henri Bergson's hand moving through the air, this is the kind of change in which there are no static positions; changing, not changed, is the reality here and it is a process without an expiry date. That is where the power of these weekly meetings seems to lie. The dominance of the Twelve Steps in addiction treatment is questioned in some quarters, for in truth there is a far from pristine success rate. Yet that sustained membership of a change community, week after week after week, seems for those who do get clean to be central to keeping the change alive. And so it would prove for Violet K.

'Yes, I had gone to NA and not,' says Violet, 'and gone and not, but to say that NA saved my life would just feel too simplistic. Desperation saved my life, that decision that I had to get clean. So I see NA not as getting me clean, but with helping me stay clean.'

Like so many of the people in this book, the early steps of change were something Violet had to choreograph for herself. She had hauled herself out of the hostel bed that bleak October day and walked to an internet café on the Earl's Court Road. There, and with some difficulty, she emailed an old friend. This was a man with whom she had done drugs some years before but who she knew was now living drug-free out on the wild west coast of Ireland. Could she visit, she wrote. For change is not only about the inner melody, as Bergson would have it, but also the external harmonies that make music of it.

'I knew I had to remove myself from my environment,' she says, 'I couldn't start again in London. It was too danger-ous. Too many triggers. So my sister bought the plane ticket to Knock and that was the beginning of my journey.' Violet pulls a little face. 'I hate that phrase really, but that was it. Because then I had to change who I was, not in essence, but a lot of muck that I'd accumulated over the years had to go.

So I went through a drug withdrawal, which was difficult, but I knew it was the end and I felt very, very safe with this man in this cottage in Connemara with his two dachshunds and burning turf on the fire. All his habits became my habits, cup of tea in the morning, making the fire, and there was just this immense vivid beauty all around me, nothing artificial. That's what I needed: reality and human connection. And I thought, *yes I can start again here. I can start again.*'

Violet says she had come back to London once early on and found herself scoring drugs within the first few hours. 'That was my last hit', she says. She flew straight back to Ireland and this time stayed for eighteen months.

In time, the euphoria of being alive and the novelty of her rural life gave way to something more grounded. 'I needed something,' says Violet, 'beyond this funny little fairyland out by the sea. I knew I wanted to build a proper life, a boyfriend, a job and now I knew what it looked like.'

Violet returned to London in late 2009 and began to train as a psychotherapist. She has been qualified for two years when this conversation takes place. One disappointment was that Sebastian did not come back to live with her, but Violet sees him most days and that, she says, is good.

As for drugs, Violet maintains she is 'very' confident that she will not slip back, 'because it's in the past and I've shut the door. It's a slow process. You know' – she searches for the words – 'you just don't do something. You don't buy drugs, you don't do drugs and it becomes easier and easier and easier. Then in time you don't want to because you find the thing that you've most been looking for anyway, which was people and intimacy and love.'

For Violet, part of that trinity of connection comes from four or five meetings at NA or AA each week, a commitment she does not anticipate tailing off, nor indeed does she wish it to. She could have put the drug habit down without NA, she says, 'But I think I would be barking mad and I think I would have probably substituted in some way, chocolate bars or men, I can't imagine.' She laughs. 'The thing is this new community replaces the people you have left behind and the twelfth step is that you pass it on. You pass on your knowledge and experience and that helps your own recovery. So I go to a meeting and I feel connected to everybody else there. I feel part of something and I come away feeling restored in some way. So why wouldn't I want to keep going back for that?'

The winter sun is now as high in the sky as it gets at this time of year. It bathes one side of Violet's face, her eyelashes turned to slivers of gold, as she blinks with concentration and considers one last question in silence. She has been asked whether having 'shut the door' means that change is ever finished, metamorphosis complete, and she has already quickly said 'No'.

'So you can't just say that was seven years ago, it's over? Why not?'

And here comes the long pause.

'Because then what?' says Violet. 'How is it over? Because it's life. It's integral. My recovery is not separate to me. People sometimes talk about their drug and alcohol recovery like it's past and I don't understand what they mean. How is it separate from their life? Because it's not external. Your recovery is in you. The change is inside and it goes on.'

18

ON LONG LIFE

The past has just happened. Right there. In the time it has taken you to turn the page from the story of Violet K. and her view of past and present, a few smithereens of the now have slipped into obsolescence. Days slip too. 'Each day we wake slightly altered', the novelist John Updike wrote in his essay *On Being a Self Forever*, 'and the person we were yesterday is dead.' Weeks, months, years, they all pass hands from what lies ahead to what is long-gone through infinitesimal increments. Yet this thought is so uncomfortable, or so poignant, that we tend to avoid thinking it. Rather, we put on, like a pair of warm slippers, an idea of the past as distantly lovely, or distantly awful, and of the future, beyond the immediately foreseeable, as an equally far-off land where you can only just make out your own small silhouette in the landscape. So remote is this Future Me ten, twenty, thirty years hence, that even though we understand that certain things will matter to him or her over there on that distant hillside, we often struggle to feel much connection or responsibility through the great wind-blown gulf in between.

According to Daphna Oyserman, a psychologist at the University of Southern California, this failure or reluctance to see current and future selves as congruent can stand in the way of our ability to make modest but life-enhancing changes. We may fail, she argues, to save for retirement, to look after our health or to study in school because of this phenomenon of 'temporal discounting', by which we attach more value to current costs and rewards than to future ones. But we do not all temporally discount to the same degree or at all times. So Oyserman set about experimenting with whether one might adjust one's sense of psychological engagement with the future, not via imaginative gymnastics down some long corridor of tomorrows, but simply by modifying the terms in which we talk about it.

What she discovered was that, in her words, 'time metrics matter'. If we simply regard future events or milestones through a 'fine-grained' time metric of days, rather than through 'gross-grained' months or years, we automatically feel a closer psychological affinity with them. That affinity, that ability to pick out the smile on the face of your Future Self over there across the valley, in turn has a palpable effect on our inclination to give that Future Self a helping hand. The irony is that this sense of continuity arguably makes us more likely to change. It makes us more likely to get planning and to take action, to start saving, to get healthy, to make whatever small push is required to give that now not so distant figure a fair shot at happiness. Try it yourself and you will find that counting your life in days, this small trick of the imagination, is a powerful change tonic.

Like the old song says, 'It's later than you think.'

Dame Gillian Lynne is on the 32,568th day of her life when she marches, bright and straight, into her swish drawing-room in Primrose Hill in London. With her precise dancer's gait, she strides to an armchair with a blue and white pouffe in front of it, which over the hours that follow she uses less for resting her feet than as a prop, a drum, a map table and a proxy for various vexing and wonderful people she has known through her long, long life. For it is long life, not overnight transformation, that concerns us here – and how to live it *well* requires a prodigious capacity for reinvention often overlooked by the rest of the world.

A world-renowned dancer and choreographer – *Cats* and *Phantom of the Opera* are two of her successes – not to mention a paragon of dynamic old age, Gillian coughs a little just as she sits down. Immediately she disappears into a monologue about why one really must not worry about this cough. She had a nasty bout of pneumonia a couple of years ago and it has left the throat 'a bit weak', she says in a strong steady voice. 'Anyway, we won't go on about that. It's just a cough. I'm fine.' You get the impression Gillian is well used to deflecting or disarming any concerns others might have for her health, any suggestion that at eighty-nine it might be time to slow down.

When you have lived as long and as vigorously as Gillian Lynne, a talent for both adaptation and continuity is woven into the very fabric of your being. Born in Bromley in 1926, her life spans not far off a century of seismic change and much more personal change besides. She often seems to talk of her life in terms of thresholds and turning-points, but she also says, 'there's a bit of me, a bit of a core, a bit of iron bar going down somewhere that hasn't changed.' Perhaps this is how it goes when one has an awful lot of life to look back on and make sense of.

The childhood Gillian describes in a little firework

display of reminiscence is full of bread and dripping teas with Mummy, woollen bathing costumes at the seaside, Shirley Temple films at the picture house. Miss Sharp's Dance Classes for Young Ladies in the ballroom of the Bell Hotel in Bromley – the family doctor's solution to her mother's concern that the eight-year-old would never, ever sit still – ignited her life's passion. 'I remember going up the big white stairs,' she says, 'and entering the ballroom and seeing all these little girls. That moment changed my life. When I entered that room I was one thing. When I left I was something else.'

At thirteen, Jill Pyrke, as she was back then, experienced what Gillian describes as 'a shattering blow which I believe has been very instructive'. In the summer of 1939 her mother was killed in a car crash. Just a few months later the world went to war, her father was called back to the army and Gillian went to live with an aunt.

'So then suddenly everything was turbulent, but I took to it a bit like a duck to water. Which is interesting, isn't it? I mean, it's an awful thing to say, but I quite liked the war.' Gillian lowers her voice and opens her pale green-grey eyes wide. 'Because since Mummy died I was lonely, so I liked the feeling of people pulling together and I was *Come on, let's get going, what can I do?* I've always had this exceptional energy, so I'd see something and throw myself into it, and I'm not sure that would've happened if there hadn't been a war and I hadn't lost my mum and my dad had been there. But I had to make a life and I'm not sure there's any other way to do it. Bravery: that's what it taught me, to say *I wonder if I could do that* and then to do it.'

The door from the kitchen opens and a small dog sprints into the room, followed by a tall man in his early sixties with a handsome shock of grey hair and a trim white beard.

'Hello, how do you do?' he says, 'I'm Peter. Cup of tea?'

'Darling,' says Gillian to him and then turns back, adding with a flash of her eyes, 'Shall we say yes?'

He puts down a plate of dainty biscuits and some little squares of cake.

'Those are for my wife. She's gluten-free, but you must have one as well.'

And he leans over to kiss Gillian, who has tilted her face up toward his, her two slender hands cupping both his cheeks.

'Now don't let the dog eat those', he says with a twinkle and departs.

'And that is also very interesting,' says Gillian in a whisper nodding towards the door that has just clicked shut, 'because I'm not sure how many women fifty-three years old who met someone of twenty-seven, which Peter was when I met him, because I was directing him in *My Fair Lady*, would then marry him. That took a lot of guts because everybody said, "Don't be so silly Gilly, you can't marry him, it's disgusting. It's disgusting at fifty-three, what's it going to be like when you're –".' Gillian does not finish this sentence, merely cocking her sandy-coloured head to one side. 'But we had taken one look at each other and we knew we were meant to be together, just like that, and I think that all this turmoil you and I have been talking about made me not afraid to leap off the high-diving board. That's very useful in the theatre and it's also quite useful in life, isn't it? It really is.'

During the war Gillian's ballet career had taken off. Anointed with a new name more suited to the billboard and chosen by her artistic director, Jill Pyrke from Bromley metamorphosed into Gillian Lynne the ballerina. Seven years with Sadler's Wells followed alongside some of the most iconic names in ballet: Margot Fonteyn, Moira Shearer, Robert Helpmann, Ninette de Valois. But, restless at Sadler's

Wells, Gillian made a transition unheard of at the time and moved into musicals. Film followed, including a brief love affair with her co-star Errol Flynn. 'I'm afraid I didn't listen to Mummy then', she says, as if this were only last week. 'I was very naughty indeed.' And suddenly the sheer stretch of this long, colourful life is palpable.

In the 1960s Gillian tried her hand at choreography and directing, uncovering a remarkable talent for both. 'Talk about change, I really did leap into thing after thing after thing', she says, making small elegant hops with her feet on the soft rug. It is to this combination of fearlessness, cheek and an elasticity of ambition that she says she owes her extraordinary career success, with, at eighty-nine, a long-running show still on Broadway, another just opened in the West End and a diary as packed as it ever was with forth-coming productions.

In Gillian Lynne you find so many of the changes that appear elsewhere in this book, from the formative trauma to the name change, from the frowned-upon love affair to the career shifts. With the hindsight of many years and the habit she says her mother instilled in her to make light of any discomfort, Gillian wears these changes with the ease of a dancer's gossamer skirts. But when you ask her if the secret of this ability to both handle change and to embrace it over the better part of a century lies in being a chameleon in some sense, she closes her big eyes for a second and shakes her head.

'Do you know, darling,' she says, 'I would love to say that, but I think I was just greedy. Honestly I've enjoyed it all so much, all this change. When I think about it, I never said no to anything. I just leaped in. Some of it was bad and some of it was brilliant, but it's gone on and on and on. And I think it's just because I look out there and I like what I see. I like life. I like people. I dive in. That's why I appear to be perhaps not quite as old as I am. Because that little kid who was so annoying, the wriggle-bum as they used to call me, I don't think that's ever quite gone. I'm restless, you see? I don't want to miss anything, and I think that that restlessness is quite useful because I do think it keeps you going. And I'm still here. I haven't lost the ability to have new ideas.' She leans sideways and touches the wood of a nearby table. 'So I think I'm very lucky that something has kept going. I don't like to say *this is how I do it*. I don't know why, darling. But I think that adaptability is probably the most important thing of the lot.'

Homo bulla. Man is a bubble, a fragile thing that lasts but a few iridescent moments. So the eighty-year-old Roman scholar Marcus Terentius Varro wrote in a letter to his wife, excusing any infelicities in the practical treatise that followed on how best to tend their lands after he had crossed the River Styx on his final journey.

Yet these days, man (and woman) is a bubble for considerably longer than in days of old. As life-expectancy has increased dramatically during the twentieth century, so the particular experience of change associated with long lives has become increasingly pertinent. As fertility rates have declined and longevity risen, the well-being of this ageing population has emerged as a field of study in its own right, one that yields many fresh insights on how we change when we grow old.

It is only in recent years that brain science has discovered how neuroplasticity, the carving out of new pathways and connections in our brains, and neurogenesis, the production of new brain cells, both continue long into adulthood and even into old age. Each is stimulated by a combination of mental and physical activity, especially that which entails a high level of concentration. Aptly, dancing, with its unique combination of mental and physical exertion, has been singled out as one of the activities associated with a lower risk of Alzheimer's, although it should be said that at this stage in research this is a correlation, not causation. What can be said for sure is that variety and activity are crucial to keeping the ageing brain as nimble as that of Gillian Lynne.

Furthermore, a limber mind combined with the unique vantage point of riper years can, for some, bring about a new kind of flourishing. The work of the psychologist and Director of the Stanford Center on Longevity, Laura Carstensen, was in part the inspiration for H'Sien Hayward's research into happiness and disability. Carstensen has worked for many years uncovering evidence of how a broad trend towards positive changes in outlook and motivation in later life – happiness by another name – are not merely the fruit of experience, of having been around the block a few times. They are also the product of our unique cognisance of time horizons, our own time horizons. Think of those portions of life spelt out in days, not years, as we saw earlier. Well, as the horizon of our own life shortens and we realise that we do not necessarily have all the time in the world, it can trigger a cascade of small metamorphoses. We realign our priorities; we sweat the small stuff a little less; we savour the things that matter to us a little more. We find that, contrary to the image of the aged in merciless decline, we grow. And we find that we are often happier in many ways than we were when, on paper at least, we were in our very prime. It is never too late to change, it seems; it is never finished. Indeed, change can invigorate us right to the very end of our lives.

On this subject, a final word from the doyen of ageing research. The Harvard psychiatrist George Vaillant – also, as it happens, doctoral supervisor to H'Sien Hayward – spent more than three decades at the helm of the longest-running and largest longitudinal biosocial study of adult development ever undertaken. Following more than 800 people, some of them over seven decades, the study generated such an extraordinary volume of data about the maturation process that the simplicity of Vaillant's two key conclusions is both surprising and beguiling. 'One', he writes, 'is that happiness is love ... The other is that ... if you follow lives long enough, people adapt and they change.'

'I do', says Gillian Lynne curtly, in reply to a question about whether she gets sick of people going on about her great age.

'Isn't it irritating?' she says, tugging impatiently at the sleeve of her workout top, '"Eighty-nine-year-old Gillian Lynne." I think to myself *Who gives a fuck whether I'm sixty, seventy, twenty or whatever I am?* I can either offer something or I can't. I'm so glad you ask that because it's such a bore. I don't think of myself as old, but I am' – she nods towards the kitchen door, where Peter can be heard tidying up the tea things – 'preparing him. Because I'm quite sure I'm going to pop off soon. I don't feel ill, but I just feel I've been so lucky to have this wonderful, long life, so full of interest. And I'm not sure how long I'll be allowed to enjoy so many things, so I say *Now, I'll probably pop off darling in the next couple of months* and I'm very practical, *I want you to make sure that the pool is clean and that you go to Pilates every day,* so I'm gradually trying to prepare him for the fact that any minute now I'm going to go whoops through there, and so he won't be ... well, of course, he'll be sad but not as devastated as if I hadn't prepared the way a bit.'

'And do you prepare yourself as well, Gillian? Can you?'

'No, I'm useless at it. I think about it. I think what will it be like, when's it going to be. But the minute I get into the rehearsal room, it goes. I forget.' Gillian Lynne beams and from the kitchen door Peter waves the receiver of the phone at her.

'Darling, your calls.'

'Anyway,' she murmurs, 'I've got to keep going until next February the 20th, when I'm ninety.' And laughing, as if at the absurdity of it all, she leaps to her feet to administer a hug by way of adieu.

19

A TANGLED BANK

Afternoon tea with Gillian Lynne leaves one unusually optimistic of the possibility, indeed the probability, of changing
in the future when life calls in one deliciously zesty way or
another. But this feeling is not the norm. Recent research
from Harvard University shows how doubtful many of us
are as to whether we will change in days or years to come.

The 2013 study, led by psychologists Jordi Quoidbach,
Daniel Gilbert and Timothy Wilson, measured the personalities, values and preferences of more than 19,000 people
between the ages of eighteen and sixty-eight, then asked how
much these people had changed in the last decade and how
much they expected to change in the decade ahead. Sure
enough, young, middle-aged and old alike all believed that
they had changed substantially in the past and their reports
tested well for objectivity and reliability. They looked back
on earlier choices – careers, partners, years of afternoon
chocolate bars, crazy tattoos – with amused bewilderment
and sometimes real regret. Yet, regardless of age, the large
majority anticipated little change in looking to the future.

Across the board, people seemed to regard the present as some kind of defining moment in which they had 'become' the person they would be for the rest of their lives. They saw themselves as *changed*, but with little capacity for *changing*.

The psychologists named it The End of History Illusion and they warned of the practical consequences, how over-estimating the stability of today can bedevil the decisions we make about tomorrow. Most intriguingly, the question of why the End of History Illusion occurs brings us back to that imaginative architecture of change we have encountered again and again through the stories in this book. On the one hand, the failure to foresee change may in part be down to our well-documented tendency to overestimate our own present qualities. There is also a stumbling block in our sense of self-knowledge, which may be undermined by entertaining the possibility of a different future me. But above all, Quoidbach, Gilbert and Wilson suggest that this extraordinary discrepancy may be down to the fact that the cognitive processes involved in reconstructing an old story are simply *easier* than those required to construct a new one. It is less taxing on the mind to revisit the past than to imagine the future.

However, if we want to change or need to change, then imagine the future we must. And if there is one thing this book has set out to do, it is to inspire and fuel a few such leaps of the imagination. So please sit back and picture this.

'I'll tell you a story that I find one of the most tragic in a way.' Tom Mitchell shifts in his seat and the leather of the chair squeaks a little. 'I was sitting on the train from Guild-ford, where I lived for a while, to London, on one of those morning commutes to the City. The conductor came on the tannoy and he said, "I'd just like to make a special mention of Mr Smith, who has been travelling on this train every Monday to Friday for forty years, to his job at ..." He mentioned a particular company. "Today is the day he's retiring, so he won't be on this train tomorrow." Everyone clapped, and I thought of this guy in his suit, every single working day for forty years, going up and down the line from Guildford to London to the same job in the same firm. Because that is my idea of perfect hell. I cannot conceive of anything more hideous than being condemned to live that sort of life. I suspect that Mr Smith would be equally appalled at the thought of tearing up his life and starting again every few years. So I suspect that change is essential for some psychologies and an absolute anathema to others. And for me, it's absolutely critical. I thrive on change. I can't live without it.'

Needless to say, Mr Mitchell does not appear to labour under the End of History Illusion. Indeed, he has a tendency to do exactly that, 'to tear up my life and start again', he says, almost as if this were beyond his control, 'often at the most inappropriate moments'. Because for Tom Mitchell change is both a way of life and the source of his most deeply held understanding of the world. His is a story in which the metamorphosis comes full circle, continuity and change, natural process and human agency join together and take flight.

At one level, Tom's predisposition towards change may be hard-wired. His father was an insatiable traveller who collected countries, according to Tom, the way some people collect ceramics or paintings. In the first twenty-one years of his life Tom moved house eighteen times.

'That sense of never having a single place that I thought of as home', he says, 'means I find it very easy to move on, both from place to place and in my life. So yes, I am my father's son. I've either inherited or assimilated his wanderlust. I can't not use my passport for more than about six weeks at a time without getting really jittery.' He smoothes his palms down the saggy arms of the chair that is wedged into one corner of his shed-cum-office as if he might be about to get up and set off right now.

The other predilection Tom inherited from the Mitchell paterfamilias was an obsession with collecting and from this would spring his other lifelong passion. It began when his mother returned from a trip to the coast with a little packet of seashells as a present for the seven-year-old Tom. He was entranced and overnight became an avid collector of seashells.

'From that day onwards', he says, 'I knew I wanted to be a biologist. I didn't even know the word evolution,' says Tom, 'but I had this intense fascination from a very early age with the minutiae of diversity.' Tom glances out of the window at a long white polytunnel in the garden outside. 'And that's still very much true to this day. I'll bore you about snowdrops a bit later.'

Sure enough, Tom went to Cambridge to read biology. When he moved on to a PhD, his research involved three six-month placements at a field centre in Brunei studying the biodiversity of the pristine rainforest there. This should have been heaven on earth for Tom, but it was not. Embroiled in a passionate relationship back in Cambridge, he missed his girlfriend achingly, which he says began to 'poison' his love of the subject. Perhaps this is why his confidence in his abilities as a scientist also started to waver.

'And I didn't want to be a second-rate academic. I either wanted to be a brilliant one', he says, 'or not an academic at all.' He shakes his head, in the way people do when they have just missed a bus. Several of Tom's friends from school had gone into the City and were living the metropolitan high-life, all taxis and parties and fine food, rather than feeling lovesick and skint in a jungle on the far side of the world. Tom limped to the end of his PhD, received his doctorate and then, as he says, he tore his life apart to start again. Within a few months Tom Mitchell was a trainee investment banker and so began a new life in the City as a high-yield bond analyst.

The sun has gone in. Tom heaves himself out of the chair and, removing a pair of muddy gardening gloves from a small electric radiator, he clicks it on.

'I hated it more or less from the start,' he says, his back still turned. 'I certainly didn't ever enjoy it.'

'Were there no good things?'

'Yeah, bonus day.'

Tom talks for some time now about how intellectually barren he found the world of finance. He says that over time the only way to survive it, for the work was gruelling in spite of the emptiness, was to count down the 365 days until bonus day, putting the money away for a gilded retirement, and to start counting again. He even made a spreadsheet that lay in a desk drawer, enumerating the days and years until he could afford to retire and never have to think about money, either earning it or making it for other people, ever again. That single thought, preceded by a pound sign, forced him onto the commuter train in the morning and got him through the fourteen-hour day that followed. He maintains that secretly a lot of people in the City think like this. Having repeatedly crunched the figures, if you can bear it, he says, it is not such a foolish calculation to make, especially in view of the inflated rewards. The only problem for Tom, and increasingly so, was the bearing it. Not every big change is wisely made.

'I had come from something', he says, 'that I thought was completely authentic. I still think that there is nothing more fascinating than the central truth about biology, the theory of evolution, and I had studied it right at the cutting edge of human understanding. Nothing gets more authentic than that. Everything after was going to be a disappointment, with hindsight.' Tom sighs so deeply that the uppermost page of a pile of papers on the floor flutters for a moment. 'But having concluded that I couldn't be part of that push at the frontiers any more, I then went into something that I was doing for entirely cynical motives. Some people are fascinated by money, but it turns out I'm not. I don't think there's anything inherently interesting about analysing financial statements and figuring out whether or not a company's credit worthy, and if so at what rate. I'm perfectly capable of doing it, but who gives a shit? Really, who gives a shit?'

Apart from counting the days, and the money, the other way Tom kept himself more or less sane during these years was by spending his salary on a succession of houses with ever larger gardens, channelling all that he missed about biology into their obsessive cultivation. He began to collect rare plants and pride himself on the diversity of his own modest and then increasingly less modest plot of green. He discovered that there were specialist nurseries – 'my pushers', he calls them – that would source and supply obscure species. The first thing he would do at the end of any working day, even after his children were born, was to head into the garden, get his hands in the soil and feel like himself again.

One of Tom Mitchell's gardens was a very long, narrow strip behind a terraced house in Clapham in London. There, on a board running right around the garden wall, Tom had painted a reminder of what really mattered, at least to him.

It was the closing passage from the first edition of Darwin's *On the Origin of Species* (1859) and for anyone interested in change, it makes powerful reading:

> It is interesting to contemplate a tangled bank, clothed with many plants of many kinds, with birds singing on the bushes, with various insects flitting about, and with worms crawling through the damp earth, and to reflect that these elaborately constructed forms, so different from each other, and dependent upon each other in so complex a manner, have all been produced by laws acting around us ... There is grandeur in this view of life, with its several powers, having been originally breathed into a few forms or into one; and that, whilst this planet has gone circling on according to the fixed law of gravity, from so simple a beginning endless forms most beautiful and most wonderful have been, and are being evolved.

Tom's love of these words would hold the key to another transformation that lay ahead, but it also speaks volumes of what had stayed the same ever since that small boy fell in thrall to nature.

Indeed, of all change narratives, evolution is surely the grandest and also the most humble. It is both simple and profoundly complex, and, however primordial in origin, it speaks of the present, of changing rather than changed. In its way, it recalls the observation with which this book began, that of Heraclitus and the river that is what it is, not in spite of change but because of it, or the beautiful butterfly whose metamorphosis depends upon continuity with that small and very hungry caterpillar.

'Those three words, "the tangled bank"', says Tom, quietly, 'they conjure for me thousands of literal and metaphorical tangled banks, full of plants and animals' – he smiles – 'and also people. It has so many ramifications, so beautiful and so profound. It explains everything. All of my passions, all of my obsessions, all of my intellectual interests are synthesised there.'

It is perhaps small wonder that in fourteen years Tom never made any close friends in banking, but he was good at the job. Clever and hard-working enough, he was also perfectly able to disport himself with what he calls 'a veneer' or sometimes 'a mask' of the projected hyper-confidence necessary within the industry to justify the substantial pay packets. Tom says it feels 'vulgar' to enumerate the sums involved, but he does mention that he was headhunted to set up a research team for Royal Bank of Scotland, a move that over the next five years 'transformed' his finances. But Tom's misery in the work itself reached new heights and eventually he says he 'started to gasp for air.' Finally, in 2008, he made the decision to quit, giving three months' notice of his intention to leave, and he set about trudging through his last days as a banker.

'I suffer from depression,' Tom says quite suddenly, running his hands through his hair. 'Have done since childhood. It comes and goes in episodes. So I think when an episode coincided with the culmination of years of living this lie, wearing this mask, and now I could see the finish line, it then just became intolerable. Something inside me snapped. I was walking to the station one day to go to work, shuffling along in this throng of commuters, and I suddenly became aware that everyone was staring at me. A concrete bollard had got in the way between me and the gates of this fucking station I had to commute from, and I was just manically kicking this bollard. I came to and realised what I was doing. I got on the train, but instead of going to work I went to see my psychiatrist and he said, "Have you ever thought you might need to step out of the world for a little while?" And I never went back to work again. That was the end.'

The painful truth is that, as for Mike Waudby or Violet K., even for the teenage Didier Long, sometimes in order to change, to be made anew, first we must break. Tom went into The Priory and emerged three weeks later to a *tabula rasa*. Yet with astonishing speed, just a couple of months, he had a plan, as if somehow half a decade of chronic unhappiness and a moment of losing it altogether was the code required to reset the system of his life. And in Tom's case that meant a return, in every sense, to first principles.

Evolution Plants is the new life that has followed, the rebuild after the reset, and it crackles with the agency and active choice that had been neutered by all those years at the (tangled) bank. A nursery for rare plant species in the rolling hills beyond the city of Bath, it is sustained by Tom's new vocation as what is called a 'plant hunter'.

'I should say that I haven't just drifted into any of this', he says flicking a thumb at the horticultural idyll outside the window. 'I decided that this is what I was going to do with the rest of my life. I very consciously made it happen. And I live in paradise in some ways now. Come on, let's have a look.'

Tom springs up from the armchair with a new energy and, at a lick, leads the way out of his office–shed, explaining how this venerable field of naturalist exploration marries all of his great passions: travel, biology, collecting, diversity. He now spends half of the year roaming the world gathering seeds of rare plant species – Turkey, Germany, Slovenia, Croatia in the last month alone – the other half of the year cultivating them.

Crunching across the gravel to a quartet of large

polytunnels and greenhouses encircled by many growing
beds, Tom says that a particular obsession has developed
with snowdrops. He slides back the plastic door of one of
the polytunnels to reveal row upon row of tiny snowdrops
in pots. It is perhaps no accident that the plant that seems
to have rescued Tom is the first hopeful flower to break the
long desolation of winter and a paragon of diversity to boot,
with many thousands of different varieties.

'There's space in the benches here for 4,000 pots of
seedlings' – he steps inside – ' So this is one of the most bio-
diverse patches of ground on the surface of the planet, more
species per unit area than the most diverse tract of rainforest
or coral reef. For a lifelong lover of diversity, it's a cathedral.'
He glances at the plastic roof, as if it were fretted with gold,
'It's the Sistine Chapel, you know? And that fills me with
joy, it really does.'

Tom says that on his gravestone should be etched a
famous quote by the biologist Theodosius Dobzhansky:
'Nothing in biology makes sense except in the light of
evolution' – but, as Tom says with a grin, 'with a little "X"
through the "in biology"'. For this would-be epitaph is the
fulcrum of his life story at so many levels and of his experience of change. Indeed, it would be tempting when writing
about him to say that Tom and the other people in this book
in some sense 'evolved', but Tom is having none of it.

'No, we haven't evolved', he says sharply; 'we've developed
or we've changed. Evolution can be a metaphor for how we
change, sure, but it's a metaphor, not biology. Having said
that, I think we do become different people. I went astray
in my twenties, but I've come back now to what I think I
should have been all along.' He straightens a potted snowdrop on the bench and then, as if it were a business card, he
hands it over. 'And I guess if this all goes tits up, what I'll
do is just tear up my life and begin again.' For the first time

today, this phrase of Tom's sounds not like an act of vandalism, but one of hope and of new possibilities.

Metamorphosis is also a biological process. Human beings evidently do not weave a pupa, liquefy their bodies inside and then re-form, emerging with an entirely new morphology. Of course we do not – any more than hungry caterpillars soul search, fall in love, find God or play the violin and then become police officers. No, metamorphosis is also a metaphor and maybe one of which the biologist in Tom Mitchell might slightly disapprove.

Yet the imagination feeds on metaphors, as caterpillars on leaves. So there may yet be worse ways of taking on our endemic doubts about change, our End of History Illusions and so many of the other imaginative obstacles that, as we have seen, we put between ourselves and the lives we want to lead.

As a way of understanding how profoundly and energetically people can and do change in the course of the same single life, metamorphosis represents a liberating idea, one embodied by each of the people we have encountered in this book. It is pragmatic and beautiful and mysterious and possible. For hunger, transformation and continuity link every one of them. These were their metamorphoses, the truth of human change out there in the real world. And if we choose to make it so, and we work hard at it, like the butterfly that kicks and writhes and shimmies from the chrysalis, it is also within our grasp.

Some months after the day at the nursery, Tom Mitchell

sent an email saying he had decided to close and sell Evolution Plants. He had mentioned before that the business was failing to make money. Not enough people want to spend £20 on an obscure variety of snowdrop; more fool them. But what could have been the devastating collapse of his dream seems for Tom to have simply sparked another new idea: to spend the coming year seeing all twenty-one species of snowdrop in flower in the wild in Azerbaijan, Iran, Russia, Armenia 'and a bunch of other interesting places', he wrote. 'Maybe I'll make a book out of it.' You could almost feel him smile from the email and it recalled something Tom had said at the end of that long afternoon amid the rows of snowdrop seedlings the former banker had grown: 'It would be a very unwise person indeed who drew lessons in wisdom from my life story. I've made more than my fair share of mistakes. I only know how I feel I must live and I couldn't live like that gentleman on the train, commuting for forty years. So I'm tempted to say that the lesson, if there is one, is to embrace change as a way of life rather than as an event or a phase transition. It's certainly a way of life for me and I don't know how to live except by embracing it wholeheartedly. That's all.'

FURTHER READING

What follows here is by no means a bibliography of past and current thinking on change. That would include more or less every novel ever written, a mountain – literally – of academic papers across the sciences and humanities, the lion's share of songs, poetry and films. Change is everywhere, once you start looking for it. So instead here is simply a taste of the sources that have stirred this book into life and which may prove of interest to those keen to delve further.

General

'The Garden of Forking Paths', Jorge Luis Borges, trans. Donald A. Yates, *Labyrinths* (Penguin, 1970)

Metamorphosis and Identity, Caroline Walker Bynum (Zone Books, 2005)

The Brain That Changes Itself, Norman Doidge (Penguin, 2007)

'Heraclitus', Daniel W. Graham, *The Stanford Encyclopedia of Philosophy*, ed. Edward N. Zalta (Fall 2015 edn)

The Philosophical Baby, Alison Gopnik (The Bodley Head, 2009)

I Am A Strange Loop, Douglas Hofstadter (Basic Books, 2007)

'The Metamorphosis', Franz Kafka, trans. Willa and Edwin Muir, *The Complete Stories* (Schocken Books, 1988)

Thinking, Fast and Slow, Daniel Kahneman (Penguin, 2012)

The Protean Self, Robert Jay Lifton (Basic Books, 1993)

The Stories We Live By, Dan P. McAdams (Guildford Press, 1997)

'Of Art and the Future', Henry Miller, *The Henry Miller Reader* (New Directions, 1969)

Ecce Homo: How One Becomes What One Is, Friedrich Nietzsche, trans. R. J. Hollingdale (Penguin Classics, 1992)

Metamorphoses, Ovid, trans. Mary M. Innes (Penguin Classics, 1980)

On Becoming a Person, Carl Rogers (Constable, 1967)

Hallucinations, Oliver Sacks (Picador, 2012)

'On Being a Self Forever', John Updike, *Self-Consciousness* (Penguin, 1990)

Identity, ed. Giselle Walker and Elisabeth Leedham-Green (Cambridge University Press, 2010)

Redirect: The Surprising New Science of Psychological Change, Timothy D. Wilson (Penguin, 2011)

Part I

Self-Efficacy, Albert Bandura (*Psychological Review*, 1977, Vol. 84)

Self-Efficacy in Changing Societies, ed. Albert Bandura (Cambridge University Press, 1995)

The Presocratic Philosophers, trans. Jonathan Barnes (Routledge, 1982)

The Helping Interview, Alfred Benjamin, 3rd edn
(Houghton Mifflin, 1981)

Outlaw, Ray Bishop (Virgin, 2014)

Self Mastery through Conscious Autosuggestion, Emile Coué
(1922)

'Umbrella Sociology', Alistair Fraser (*International Institute
of Asian Studies Newsletter*, No. 70, Spring 2015)

Gallup's *State of the Global Workplace* report (2013) can be
found at http://www.gallup.com/services/178517/state-
global-workplace.aspx

*We Wish To Inform You That Tomorrow We Will Be Killed
With Our Families*, Philip Gourevitch (Picador, 2000)

Genocide in Rwanda, April–May 1994, Human Rights
Watch/Africa (Vol. 6, No. 4, 1994)

Principles of Psychology, William James (Henry Holt, 1890)

'Possible Selves', Hazel Markus and Paula Nurius (*American
Psychologist*, Vol. 41, 1986)

*Making Good: How Ex-Convicts Reform and Rebuild
Their Lives,* Shadd Maruna (American Psychological
Association, 2007)

'Discovering Desistance', Prof. Fergus McNeill's blog,
http://blogs.iriss.org.uk/discoveringdesistance/author/
fergusmcneill/

The Sociological Imagination, Charles Wright Mills (Oxford
University Press, 2000)

Why Grow Up?, Susan Neiman (Penguin, 2014)

Metamorphosis, Frank Ryan (One World, 2011)

Pensées, Blaise Pascal, trans. A. J. Krailsheimer (Penguin
Classics, 1995)

Part II

Where is the Mango Princess?, Cathy Crimmins (Vintage,
2002)

Sexual Fluidity: Understanding Women's Love and Desire,
  Lisa M. Diamond (Harvard University Press, 2009)
Why We Love, Helen Fisher (Holt McDougal, 2005)
Modernity and Self-Identity, Anthony Giddens (Polity
  Press, 1991)
A Treatise of Human Nature, David Hume, ed. Ernest
  Mossner (Penguin Classics, 1985)
'Habit', William James (Henry Holt, 1914), https://archive.
  org/details/habitjam00jameuoft
The Secret Life of Houdini, William Kalush and Larry
  Sloman (Scribner, 2007)
A General Theory of Love, Thomas Lewis, Fari Amini and
  Richard Lannon (Vintage, 2005)
Plutarch's *Lives*, trans. John Dryden, ed. Arthur Hugh
  Clough (Modern Library, 2001)
The Strange Case of Dr Jekyll and Mr Hyde, Robert Louis
  Stevenson (Penguin Classics, 2002)
Mike Waudby's website is www.theweightlosswarriors.co.uk
  and includes a link to his e-book about his experiences.

Part III

The Nicomachean Ethics, Aristotle, trans. J. A. K. Thomson
  (Penguin Classics, 2004)
'The Anatomy of Stages of Change', editorial by Albert
  Bandura (*American Journal of Health Promotion*, Vol.
  12, 1997)
Winter Notes on Summer Impressions, Fyodor Dostoevsky,
  trans. Kyril FitzLyon (Alma Classics, 2008)
A Theory of Cognitive Dissonance, Leon Festinger (Stanford
  University Press, 1957)
When Prophecy Fails, Leon Festinger, Henry W. Riecken
  and Stanley Schachter (Pinter & Martin, 2008)
Man's Search for Meaning, Viktor E. Frankl (Rider, 2004)
Stasiland, Anna Funder (Granta, 2011)

Ich folgte den falschen Göttern, Salomea Genin (Verlag für Berlin-Brandenburg, 2012)

Shattered Assumptions, Ronnie Janoff-Bulman (Simon & Schuster, 1992)

Memories, Dreams, Reflections, Carl Jung (Fontana, 1995)

Inside the Jihad, Omar Nasiri (Basic Books, 2008)

Plato's *Republic*, trans. Desmond Lee (Penguin Classics, 2007)

C. G. Jung Speaking, ed. William McGuire and R. F. C. Hull (Picador, 1980)

'Paradoxical Effects of Thought Suppression', D. M. Wegner et al. (*Journal of Personality and Social Psychology*, Vol. 53, 1987)

Part IV

The Big Book, Alcoholics Anonymous (Hazelden Publishing, 2002)

'The Perception of Change', Henri Bergson, *Key Writings*, ed. Keith Ansell Pearson and John Ó Maoilearca (Bloomsbury, 2002)

A Long Bright Future, Laura L. Carstensen (Crown, 2009)

On the Origin of Species, Charles Darwin (Oxford University Press, 2008)

An Essay Concerning Human Understanding, John Locke (Wordsworth, 2014)

A Dancer in Wartime, Gillian Lynne (Vintage, 2011)

The Black Mirror, Raymond Tallis (Atlantic, 2015)

Triumphs of Experience, George E. Vaillant (Harvard University Press, 2015)

ACKNOWLEDGEMENTS

Thinking and writing about change for many months has been a transformative experience in itself. I am thankful to a great many people for making the process so rich and so revelatory, but above all I owe a huge debt of gratitude to those whose stories feature here – for their time and for answering my impertinent questions with staggering honesty and insight. *Metamorphosis* is their book and it has been a delight and an inspiration to spend time with them.

Heartfelt thanks to all the team at Profile Books, including Andrew Franklin, Penny Daniel, Daniel Crewe, Pete Dyer, Steve Panton, Patrick Taylor, Simon Shelmerdine, Claire Beaumont, Anna-Marie Fitzgerald, Flora Willis and above all, my editor, Rebecca Gray. Her combination of cool intelligence and warm humanity – not to mention a willingness to jot the odd cuss-word in the margin of my manuscript – have become a pillar of my writing life over the last six years. The other constant has been my wonderful agent, Patrick Walsh, for whom I thank my lucky stars daily. His contributions are too many and too various to enumerate, but I am deeply indebted to him and to his brilliant team at Conville and Walsh.

Acknowledgements

I also wish to thank the following people who have helped in many ways, practically and editorially, at home and overseas: Jane Alcala, April Benson, Samantha Bessis, Professor Gary Bruce, Professor Katra Byram, Marion Cole, Belle Beth Cooper, Sandra Down, Tony Eldridge, Mattie Faint, Harriet Fletcher, Professor Elana Gomel, Sarah Gray, James Greenwood, Lois Harris, Clare Hazeldine, Ophelia Hogan, Professor Timothy L. Jackson, Margaret Kelly, Melissa and Jamie Learmond, Quentin Letts, Professor Janina Levin, Adrian Levy, Katherine Lynch, Anne and Jim McLean, Professor Tariq Modood, Nick Morland, Professor Ellen Peel, Emma Piesse, Cathy Scott-Clark, Sarah Selby, Haran Sivapalan, Edward Thornton, Kristin Tomlinson, Katy and Kevin Whelan, Mick Yates.

Especial thanks go to Louise and Andrew Frankel for giving me the perfect hideaway in which to write; to Professor Fergus McNeill for sharing his captivating work on criminal desistance and to Jude Allen, Shera Bathurst, Alan Jackson, Noel Smith, Rachel Smith at Headway and Tessa Williams for directing me towards specific stories that appear in these pages.

Finally, Henry has lived with this book as long as I have and has done so with an equanimity that has been frankly heroic. Meanwhile our sons, Sam, Milo and Freddie, have buoyed me up with tales of leopards that change their spots and caterpillars that take to the wing, their confidence that any of us can change if we want to enough, both refreshing and inspiring. Because, of course, they are right.